EGYPTIAN MUMMIES

EGYPTIAN MUMMIES

JOHN H. TAYLOR

Published in co-operation with British Museum Press
UNIVERSITY OF TEXAS PRESS, AUSTIN

First published in 2010 by The British Museum Press
A division of The British Museum Company Ltd
38 Russell Square
London WC1B 3QQ

First University of Texas Press edition, 2010
ISBN-10: 0-292-72586-8
ISBN-13: 978-0-292-72586-7

Library of Congress Control Number: 2010929878

Designed by Zoë Mellors
Printed in China

Frontispiece
Mummy of Cleopatra, daughter of Soter. From Thebes, early second century AD.
Length 1.68 m (see page 42).

Page 5
Painted wooden model of a funerary boat. From Thebes, 12th Dynasty, c.1850 BC.
Length 77.5 cm (see page 117).

Note about images
The vast majority of objects illustrated in this book are from the collections
of the British Museum. The British Museum object registration numbers are listed
on page 160. For further reading and web resources, please see page 155.

CONTENTS

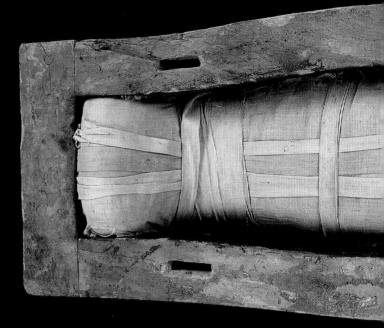

CHAPTER I

INTRODUCTION

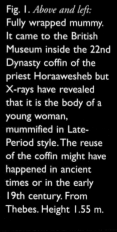

Fig. 1. *Above and left:* Fully wrapped mummy. It came to the British Museum inside the 22nd Dynasty coffin of the priest Horaawesheb but X-rays have revealed that it is the body of a young woman, mummified in Late-Period style. The reuse of the coffin might have happened in ancient times or in the early 19th century. From Thebes. Height 1.55 m.

MANY SOCIETIES, ANCIENT AND MODERN, have performed special treatments on the bodies of the dead, but it is with ancient Egypt that artificial preservation of the corpse is most closely associated.

Thousands of Egyptian mummies have been discovered, and many of these can be seen in museums, not only in Egypt itself but in every part of the world. Mummification has enabled us to look into the faces of figures from the remote past and to see them as recognizable fellow human beings. For the historian and the scientist, mummies are a priceless storehouse of factual information about past societies. The study of mummies can fill in gaps in our knowledge on subjects which written and graphic sources tell us little about: life expectancy, nutrition, health, disease and embalming techniques. But it was not the Egyptians' intention to leave a legacy for future generations. In preserving the dead, they strove to ensure their own immortality by enabling them to enter the afterlife.

Mummies – human remains in which soft tissues are preserved as well as bones – owe their existence both to natural phenomena such as extremes of heat and cold and to artificial methods which were

Fig. 2. *Above:* Head of the mummy of King Sety I. With minimal distortion to the facial features, this is one of the highest achievements of ancient embalmers. From Deir el-Bahri. 19th Dynasty, c.1279 BC.

deliberately applied to prevent decomposition. Ancient Egypt stands alone in carrying out this practice to such a high standard and for so long a period of time. Attempts at mummification in Egypt are known from as early as the middle of the fourth millennium BC and the practice continued as late as the third or fourth century AD – a time-span of nearly 4,000 years. The word 'mummy' comes from the old Persian *mummia*, 'bitumen'. The term was applied in the middle ages to the embalmed bodies of ancient Egyptians because the blackened appearance of the skin – a frequent side-effect of the application of resin – was thought to have been caused by the use of bitumen in their preservation (see page 142). In fact, real bitumen was not extensively used in mummification until a relatively late date, but the name has now passed into regular usage in the major European languages: English *mummy,* French *momie,* and German *Mumie.*

The religious background to mummification

In some societies it has been thought that the bodies of the dead had to be consumed by fire, natural decay or animal activity in order for the spirit to be released to enter a new life. But the Egyptians held a directly opposite view. According to their beliefs the preservation of the body was essential if life after

Fig. 3. *Below:* Nesitanebisheru seated before a table of food offerings for her spirit. The tables take the form of the hieroglyph *ka* (a pair of arms bent upwards at the elbows), which symbolizes the connection between the *ka* and provision of sustenance for the dead. *Book of the Dead* on papyrus, from Deir el-Bahri. Early 22nd Dynasty, *c.*930 BC. Height 52 cm.

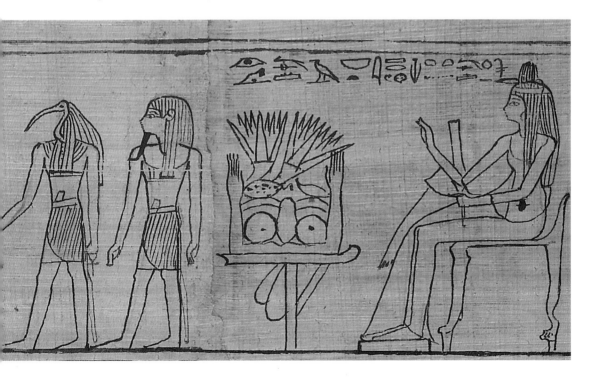

Fig. 4. *Right:* Steatite shabti figure of the Master of Horse Sunur, intended to act as a substitute which would work on behalf of its owner in the afterlife (see page 122). Here, Sunur is embraced by his *ba*, the freely-moving spirit form in which he would be able to leave and re-enter his tomb after death. Provenance unknown. 19th Dynasty, *c.*1275 BC. Height 21.4 cm.

death was to be attained. Their writings show that a person was believed to be made up of different constituent elements. The Egyptian word for them was *kheperu,* which can be translated as 'manifestations' or 'modes of existence'. The body itself was one of these, as were the heart, the name, and the shadow. Especially important were the non-physical aspects of the person, the spirits known as the *ka* and the *ba*. Both of these have been compared with the modern western notion of the soul, but a simple bipartite division into body and spirit does not reflect the complexity of the Egyptians' concept of the individual.

During a person's life the *ka* was a kind of spiritual counterpart, a vital force which linked the person with past generations; after death it remained in the grave or tomb, where it was nourished with offerings of food and drink. The *ba,* a more independent spirit, could eat, drink, speak and move through its own power. The ability to move freely was one of its main characteristics, and for this reason it was represented as a human-headed bird. However, neither the *ka* nor the *ba* could exist independently for ever. They required a physical form to inhabit. For the *ka* this was usually a statue of the owner; for the *ba* it was the mummy that provided the physical 'anchor'; although the *ba* could leave the tomb by day, it was vitally important that it should return at night to be reunited with the mummy.

While a person was alive the body acted as the focal point of all these modes of existence, but at death the connection between them was broken and they became independent. Only by restoring the unity between a person's component parts could life be renewed, and this was the chief aim of the mortuary practices of the ancient Egyptians. Not surprisingly, care for the body was central to their beliefs. If the corpse were destroyed the *ba* would be unable to reunite itself with its physical base, and the person would cease to exist. So proper disposal of the dead was considered to be of the greatest importance.

At the most basic level this meant burial in a pit-grave scooped out of the sand, which protected the corpse from the elements and from attack by insects and scavenging animals. With the passage of time it came to be thought desirable that the remains of the dead should be transformed into a more perfect body, suitable for eternal life. In this way artificial mummification arose.

The afterlife expected by most Egyptian peasants was not described in inscriptions or represented in art, because only the elite members of society were literate and were able to afford the texts and religious images which provide most of our information on this subject. But the simple objects found in the graves of the poor offer clues. From them we can deduce that they expected to enter an existence that was broadly similar to the earthly life, one in which food, drink and clothing would still be needed, as well as tools, weapons and items of bodily

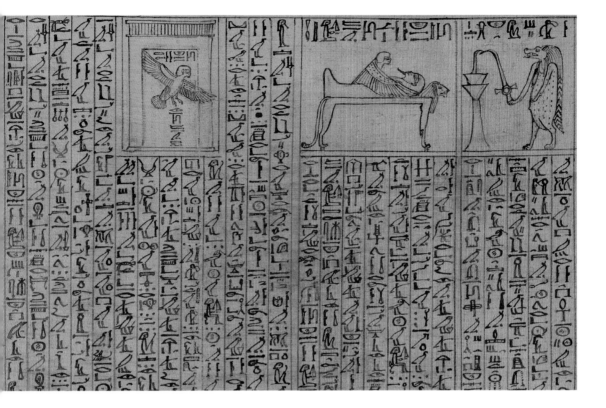

Fig. 5. *Above:* Two vignettes from the *Book of the Dead* papyrus of the draughtsman and temple copyist Nebseny, details of which are shown on page 13. At far right, the hippopotamus goddess Ipy lights a torch to protect the deceased. From the Memphite necropolis. 18th Dynasty, *c.*1400 BC. Height 35.8 cm.

adornment. The same concern for provisioning the dead with basic human necessities is seen in the texts and images found in the tombs of the wealthy, but here the afterlife is firmly set within a religious context. During the three millennia of the pharaonic period (*c.*3000–30 BC) the Egyptians developed a number of different concepts of human existence after death. These ideas were sometimes contradictory and they were never fully synthesized into a single, consistent mythology, but a common element of all of the concepts was the idea that to achieve resurrection the deceased must become more closely integrated into the natural processes of the cosmos. The motions of the sun, moon and stars, the yearly flooding of the Nile and the constant renewal of vegetation were viewed as signs of an eternal cycle of creation, into which human life was inextricably bound. In Egyptian mythology, the creative power that brought the renewal of life was closely associated with the gods Osiris and Ra.

The story of Osiris was one of the most powerful myths in ancient Egyptian tradition. Osiris was said to have been a wise and beneficent king of Egypt in the legendary past, but his jealous brother Seth murdered him in order to take his place. Osiris's body was cut to pieces and scattered throughout Egypt, but Isis, his sister and wife, gathered up the fragments. They were joined together and bound in wrappings by the embalmer-god Anubis, and Osiris was brought back to life to become ruler of the *Duat* or netherworld, the realm inhabited by the dead. Meanwhile, his son Horus defeated Seth and ascended the throne on earth. Mummification began in Egypt centuries before parts of this myth were first written down, but the story provided a mythological rationale for the artificial preservation and wrapping of the bodies of the dead, and from the Middle Kingdom (*c*.2125–1650 BC) onwards Osiris was usually depicted as a shrouded figure resembling a mummy. By his example, Osiris offered to every Egyptian the hope of resurrection after death, and so in the rituals of burial the deceased was closely associated with the god and his or her name was preceded by the title 'the Osiris'.

The sun god Ra was regarded as the creator of the world and all living creatures. Unlike Osiris, he did not meet a violent end, but he did experience a symbolic 'death' each evening at sunset. During the hours of night the sun god was believed to travel through the netherworld, fighting against the forces of chaos which tried to overthrow *Maat*, the Egyptians' name for the principle of order and right by which the cosmos was maintained. When he reappeared on the eastern horizon at dawn the god had undergone rejuvenation. The *Books of the Netherworld*, carved and painted on the walls of royal tombs in the Valley of the Kings, describe this process, explaining that during the night the spirit of the sun god met his own corpse, which was equated with Osiris. This joining of the

Fig. 6. *Below:* Details of fig. 5. On the left Nebseny's *ba* as a human-headed bird flies through the entrance to his tomb, the vignette of spell 92 of the *Book of the Dead*. On the right the *ba* has returned to the tomb to embrace the mummified body of Nebseny which lies on a lion-shaped bier, from spell 89.

Fig. 7. *Right:* The union of the *ba* and the mummy was believed to be crucial to the survival of the person after death. On the interior of the coffin of the priest of Amun, Bakenmut the *ba* is represented with its wings outspread as if descending to embrace the body. Wooden coffin; painted detail on plaster. From Deir el-Bahri. Late 21st Dynasty, *c.*975 BC. Height 208.4 cm.

two most important manifestations of the deity ensured that the life-cycle of both gods would be repeated every day, and hence life on earth would continue. In this way, two different myths were skilfully woven together, and the meeting of Ra and Osiris served as the divine model for the joining of the mortal *ba* with the mummy.

The ultimate aim of the deceased Egyptian was to enter the netherworld, where he or she would themselves have some of the powers and characteristics of gods. This elevated and eternal state of being was called *akh,* a word which had connotations of luminosity and the possession of creative power. A person who had achieved this was himself called an *akh,* and this term is sometimes listed among the modes of existence in ancient texts although one could not be an *akh*

Fig. 8. *Left:* Sokar-Osiris, a composite deity who combined features of the Memphite funerary god Sokar with Osiris, the ruler of the netherworld. *Book of the Dead,* papyrus of Nodjmet, from Deir el-Bahri. Early 21st Dynasty, c.1050 BC. Height 34 cm.

Fig. 9. *Right:* Schist group-statue representing the god Osiris protected by the wings of his wife Isis. Osiris wears a crown adorned with ostrich feathers and grasps the royal sceptres, the crook and flail, denoting his status as ruler of the realm of the dead. From Karnak. 26th Dynasty, c.550 BC. Height 81 cm.

during the life on earth. To reach this state after death, many preconditions had to be fulfilled: not only special treatment of the corpse (including mummification), but the construction of a permanent resting-place (the tomb), and the establishment of a funerary cult to keep the dead person alive. The rituals which were performed on behalf of the dead were called *sakhu*, literally 'that which makes [a person] an *akh*'.

Only the wealthiest Egyptians possessed the means to pay for the more elaborate versions of mummification, involving lengthy desiccation of the corpse, anointing with costly oils and spices and special treatment of the internal organs. Poorer people might not be able to afford this method, but even they were wrapped in linen, their swathed bodies bearing a superficial resemblance to the pampered corpses of their social superiors. Having one's remains treated in this way was more than just an aspiration to high rank. Mummification was perceived as a defining mark of being Egyptian. The ancient Egyptians were very conscious of their own collective identity, and their distinctive burial practices were one way in which this was expressed. In the literary text known as the *Story of Sinuhe* an Egyptian who has lived abroad in exile for many years is urged to return home with the promise of a proper Egyptian burial, 'with oils, and wrappings from the hands of Tayet [goddess of weaving] … a mummy-case of gold, a mask of lapis lazuli …'. This ideal is contrasted with the method of disposing of the dead among foreigners: 'Asiatics shall not inter you. You shall not be wrapped in the skin of a ram to serve as your coffin.' Mummification thus confirmed that one was Egyptian, and foreign elites who wished to pose as Egyptians (such as the Libyans and Kushites who ruled Egypt in the first millennium BC) adopted this custom, together with other traditional funerary practices associated with it. Even those who did not partake of this elaborate treatment of the dead were struck by its strangeness. The Greeks and Romans were particularly fascinated by the custom and deliberately sought out information on the subject. What they recorded has turned out to be immensely useful in understanding and reconstructing the practical procedures involved in making a mummy. The following chapters describe how the body was embalmed, the trappings which were placed upon it, and the role of tombs, coffins and rituals in enabling the deceased to pass safely from earthly life, through death to the afterlife.

Fig. 10. *Below:*
An extract from the *Book of Amduat*, describing the
journey of the sun god Ra through the netherworld
during the twelve hours of the night. The god, in his
nocturnal shape as a ram-headed man, stands in his
barque, which is towed by deities to the horizon. At far
right, the scarab beetle Khepri propels the sun disc into
the sky, where it is raised up on the arms of the god
Shu. Papyrus of Ankhefenkhons, from Thebes. Late 21st
or early 22nd Dynasty, *c*.970–900 BC. Height 20 cm.

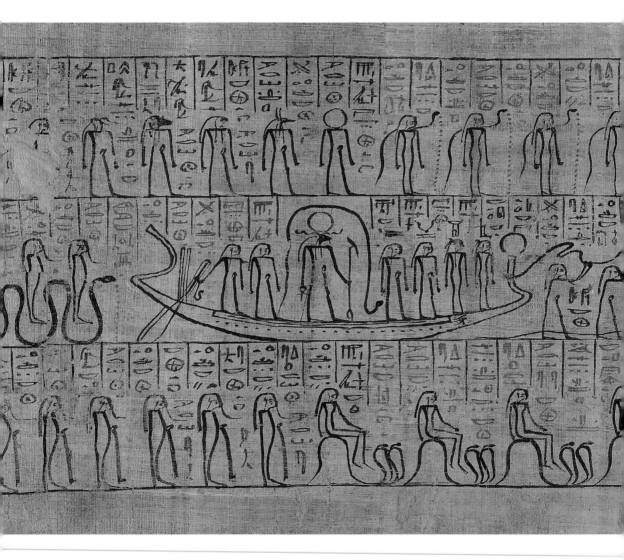

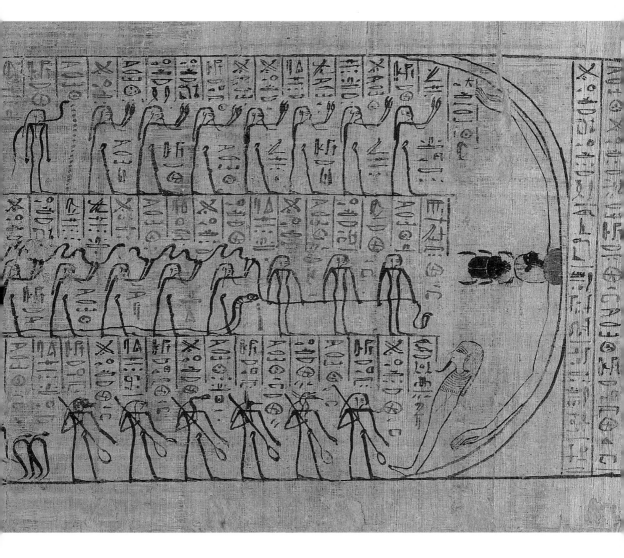

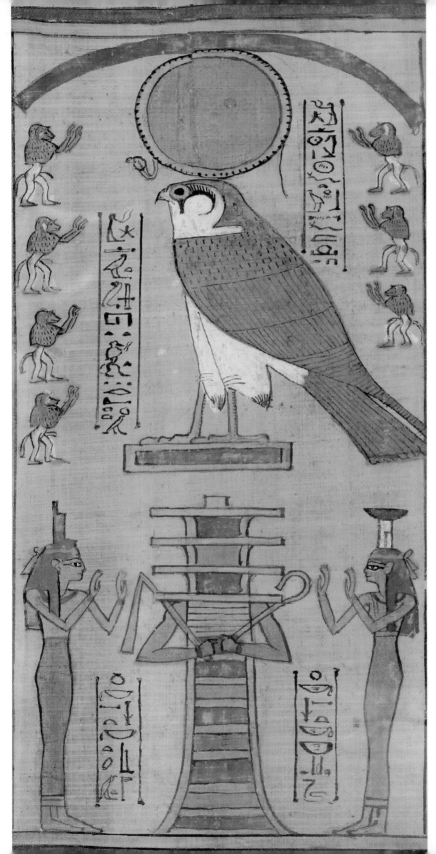

Fig. 11. *Far left:*
The union of the sun god Ra with Osiris in the netherworld is encapsulated in a single figure, painted on a wall of the tomb of Nefertari, wife of Ramesses II. The ram-head of the sun god is merged with the shrouded body of Osiris, and the hieroglyphic texts explain that each god is 'at rest' in the other. The unified deity is protected by Isis and Nephthys. Valley of the Queens, Thebes. 19th Dynasty, c.1260 BC.

Fig. 12. *Left:*
A symbolic image of the sunrise. The sun god in the form of a falcon wearing the solar disc as a headdress is depicted above the *djed*-pillar. The pillar personifies the god Osiris, ruler of the netherworld. Baboons acclaim the rising sun and the sister goddesses Isis and Nephthys protect and worship Osiris. From the *Book of the Dead,* papyrus of Hunefer. Thebes, 19th Dynasty, c.1280 BC. Height 39 cm.

CHAPTER 2

THE PROCESS OF MUMMIFICATION

Fig. 13. *Above:*
Paintings from the
lid of the coffin of
Djedbastetiufankh. The
mummy, wrapped in
bandages, is attended by
Anubis (right). At left,
the body lies on a bier,
beneath which are the
four canopic jars. From
el-Hibeh. Late Period,
c.600–300 BC. Height
of coffin 177 cm.

Hail to you, my father Osiris! You shall possess your body; you shall not become corrupt, you shall not have worms, you shall not be distended, you shall not stink, you shall not become putrid.

THESE WORDS FROM SPELL 154 of the *Book of the Dead* are typical of many passages from Egyptian funerary texts. They show that the Egyptians, like most societies, were repelled by the effects of the decay of the body after death. Their mortuary rituals sought to frustrate these abhorrent processes, and mummification came to be regarded as highly important. The commonest ancient Egyptian word for mummy was *sah*, which is closely related to a word meaning 'noble'. It reflected the idea that through the rituals of death the individual had been separated from all that was unclean and disgusting and raised to high status. Mummification also aimed to transform the corpse into a new body, one that was composed of divine substances – beautiful, shining and sweet-smelling like the body of a god.

The evidence

The ancient Egyptians themselves have left very little written or pictorial evidence about the methods which they used to preserve dead bodies. Mummification was accompanied by rituals and access to details of the procedures was probably restricted. In an inscription in the tomb of Sabni at Aswan (6th Dynasty) the specialist knowledge of the embalmers is referred to as their 'secrets', and at this period the chief embalmer held the title *hery seshta*, 'master of secrets'. A few documents which describe some aspects of Egyptian embalming have nonetheless come down to us. One of these, Papyrus Rhind I, written about the end of the first century BC, mentions many of the key stages in mummification, but the emphasis is on the religious background to the process. Another text, the *Ritual of Embalming*, which survives in incomplete form on several hieratic papyri of the Roman Period, provides instructions for the wrapping of the body and the placing of amulets with appropriate incantations, but again ignores the practical aspects of the work. It is possible that the procedures were never written down, being perhaps passed on by word of mouth. Depictions of mummification in tomb chapels and on papyri almost invariably show the body after the completion of the process, fully wrapped and attended by the jackal-headed embalmer god Anubis. Images placed in the tomb were believed to have the power to become reality, so to depict the gruesome details of the evisceration and drying of the corpse would have been thought inappropriate

Fig. 14. *Opposite:* In this rare depiction of mummification the corpse, portrayed as a silhouette, undergoes two cleansings or anointings (lower scene). In the scene above it lies on a lion-shaped table, the head supported by a headrest. The table is approached by a group of embalmers, led by a figure representing the god Anubis. See page 23 for details of the top scene and provenance.

24

and perhaps even dangerous. Exceptionally, three wooden coffins from el-Hibeh, dating to about 500 BC, have painted scenes of mummification, but even here the only stages shown are the naked corpse being purified with liquids and then lying on a lion-shaped table at the beginning of the embalming.

The most detailed written evidence for the practices of the embalmers comes from the Greek historians Herodotus and Diodorus Siculus. Herodotus gathered his information on a visit to Egypt about 450 BC, and Diodorus wrote during the first century BC. Both of them, therefore, describe a relatively late form of mummification, over two thousand years after it had begun, but their accounts contain numerous specific details which are not recorded anywhere else. The facts given in these Classical sources agree closely with evidence from the mummies themselves. Indeed it is from examinations of actual mummies, both by unwrapping and by non-invasive methods, that much of the current knowledge of Egyptian embalming has been obtained. Scientific analysis of embalming materials has thrown new light on the preservative substances which were available to the Egyptians and the manner in which they used them. In addition, tools or equipment belonging to the embalmers have occasionally been found in or near tombs, as has the refuse left over after mummification. Experiments aimed at replicating the ancient processes have also added to knowledge. Several of these 'modern mummifications' have been carried out on the bodies of small animals and birds, and in 1994 a complete human body was embalmed according to Egyptian practices. It is clear from all these sources of evidence that the formal treatment of the dead body changed over time, and also that different procedures were in use simultaneously. These variations probably reflected the wealth and status of the individual, the fashions of different geographical regions or the working practices of distinct groups of embalmers.

Fig. 15. *Opposite:* The standard image of mummification in Egyptian art shows the fully-wrapped mummy lying on a lion-shaped bier and attended by the god Anubis. In this depiction, from the limestone pyramidion of Wedjahor, the four canopic jars are represented beneath the bier, while Isis and Nephthys stand at each end protecting the deceased. At the top Anubis appears again in jackal-form and provided with royal sceptres. From Abydos. 26th Dynasty, c.630 BC. Height 61 cm.

27

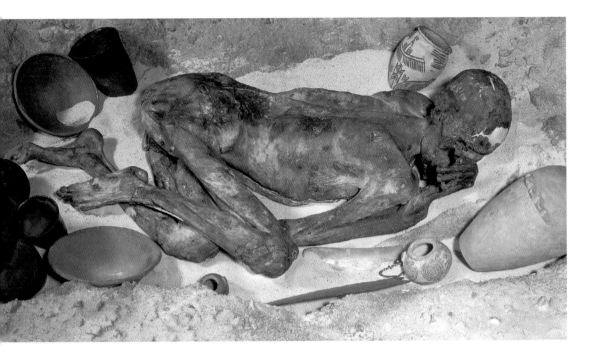

Fig. 16. *Above:* The naturally preserved remains of a man who was buried in a simple pit-grave. The stone and pottery vessels, flint knives, beads and mudstone palette laid around him come from other graves, but are typical burial goods of the period. Found at Gebelein, Upper Egypt. Late Predynastic Period, c.3400 BC. Length of body 163 cm.

A history of mummification

The earliest mummification in Egypt was a purely natural process which occurred spontaneously. In the Predynastic Period (before about 3000 BC), the dead were simply buried in pits scooped out of the desert sand. A few gifts and possessions were placed beside them (an indication, in this pre-literate period, that some form of afterlife was expected), and the grave was filled with sand and perhaps marked with stones or some simple monument. Thousands of graves of this type have been excavated by archaeologists. In most of them the flesh had decayed, and only the skeleton remained, but sometimes the bodies are found in a remarkable state of preservation. An example of this type of burial was found at Gebelein in Upper Egypt. It is that of a man who probably lived around 3400 BC (fig. 16). The state of development of his bones and the condition of his teeth suggest that he died in his thirties (aged between 30–35), but his name will never be known because he lived before the invention of writing. The hot dry sand which filled the grave had rapidly drawn out all the fluids from his body, preventing the enzymatic and bacterial activity and insect attack which would otherwise have destroyed the soft tissues. The man's bones are still covered with skin, his muscle fibres remain strong, his curly reddish hair is clearly visible, and his finger and toe nails are still lifelike.

The preservation of the man from Gebelein was accidental, but discoveries at other sites have shown that even at this early date some bodies were receiving special treatment which foreshadowed the mummification processes of later centuries. Linen wrappings impregnated with resin from coniferous trees and plants have been found in graves at Badari and Mostagedda, and may be dated as early as 4500–4100 BC. At Hierakonpolis, the centre of an important political entity in the late fourth millennium BC, bodies have been found on which areas of the head, neck and hands had been coated with pads of linen soaked in resin, enabling the cloth to be moulded to the contours of the limbs. In some cases it even seems that the internal organs were deliberately extracted and wrapped before being replaced in the chest. One corpse was covered with an aromatic tree-bark which may have been frankincense or myrrh. These discoveries are the first clear indications of deliberate attempts at artificial mummification in Egypt. Evidence of this proto-mummification has been found in a cemetery for high status members of society at Hierakonpolis, but the best examples discovered there so far are the bodies of people of fairly humble rank, which show that the practice was not restricted to the elite. It is not yet clear how widespread these treatments were at this early period, or whether the aim was to achieve full preservation of the corpse or simply to protect areas such as the hands and mouth, which may have been considered important because of their role in feeding oneself.

During the following centuries many people of lower rank continued to be buried without artificial preservation. Some form of mummification was however practiced at this time. Fragments from the royal tombs of the 1st Dynasty at Abydos show that the bodies there were wrapped in resin-impregnated linen, sometimes up to 100 layers in thickness, but it is not until the early years of the

Fig. 17. *Below:*
A mummy of the Old Kingdom discovered at Meidum in 1891. It was wrapped in many layers of linen, the outermost of which were soaked with resin and moulded into the shape of the body. The limbs, facial features and genitals were skilfully delineated, and the eyes, eyebrows and moustache were added in paint. The body was filled with resin-soaked linen. Formerly kept in the Royal College of Surgeons, London, the mummy was destroyed by bombing in 1941. The image below is reproduced from an old photograph of which no digital record exists.

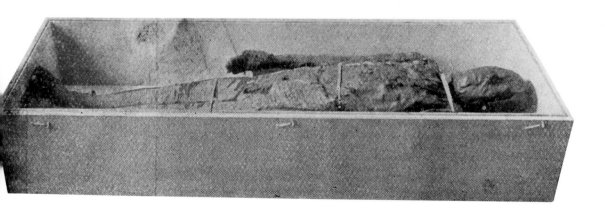

Fig. 18. *Right (detail):* Unwrapped mummy of an unidentified woman. The well-preserved body shows the incision made by the embalmers in the left side of the abdomen, through which the internal organs, with the exception of the heart, were extracted and separately preserved. The surface of the skin has been coated with resin and threads have been wound around the fingers to prevent the loss of the nails during tissue-shrinkage. From Thebes. 26th Dynasty, c.650 BC. Length of mummy 1.52 m.

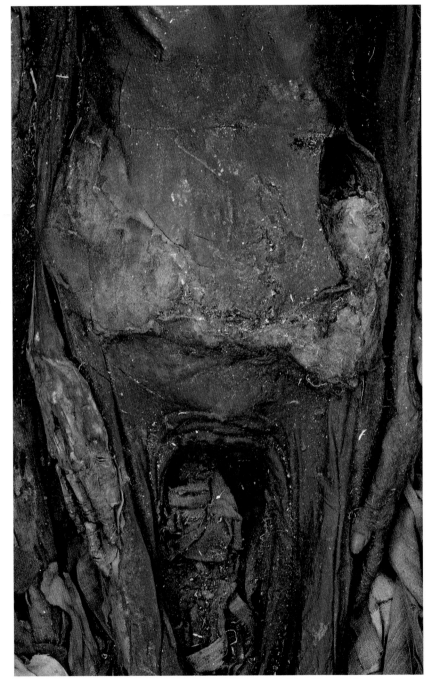

Old Kingdom (*c.*2600 BC) that significant developments in embalming procedures can be clearly detected. It has been supposed that after about 3000 BC the growing custom of placing the body in a coffin or a burial chamber with walls of brick or wood motivated the Egyptians to improve mummification techniques, because the coffin and chamber isolated the corpse from the hot sand so that it no longer acted as a natural preservative. There may be some truth in this, but it is clear that primitive mummification had begun in Egypt even before the first coffins and formal tombs were made.

One of the most important developments in the Old Kingdom (about 2682–2181 BC) was the establishment of the practice of extracting the internal organs as a regular feature of mummification. The Egyptians must have realized that these were the first parts of the body to decay after death and that, unless they were removed without delay, putrefaction would spread rapidly throughout the corpse. The viscera were therefore removed from the chest and abdomen and preserved separately. The tomb of Queen Hetepheres, wife of King Sneferu (*c.*2600 BC), contained a calcite box divided into four compartments to receive her preserved internal organs. These had been treated with natron, a natural salt which was to become the main dehydration agent in later mummification.

At the same period the position of the body in the grave began to be changed. In earlier times the arms and legs were bent, with the hands in front of the face and the knees drawn up to the abdomen, a posture resembling both a child in its mother's womb and a sleeping person (possibly reflecting ideas that the dead

Fig. 19. *Left:* Linen package containing crystalline natron salts. Large numbers of these bags were inserted into the thoracic and abdominal cavities, while loose natron was heaped over the corpse. The dry salts would absorb the body's fluids, desiccating it. From Deir el-Bahri. Probably Third Intermediate Period, *c.*1069–664 BC. 14.8 cm x 11.6 cm.

31

Fig. 20. *Above:* Pottery vessels, used to hold oils and other preservative substances which were employed in mummification. From Saqqara and other sites, 26th Dynasty (664–525 BC) or later. Height of largest vessel 10 cm.

would be reborn or would awake from the 'sleep' of death). During the Old Kingdom it became common practice for the body to be prepared for burial with the legs fully extended and the arms placed at the sides. This arrangement seems to have come into fashion at about the same time as the custom of eviscerating the corpse, perhaps because that operation would be more easily performed on an extended body.

Few mummies survive from the Old Kingdom, but those that have been found show that several different methods of treating the body were in use. Some corpses were simply swathed in many layers of linen, while in other cases the surface of the skin was coated with gypsum plaster or with linen soaked in molten resin. The facial features and other parts of the body were carefully modelled in situ in these media, and details of eyes and eyebrows were added in paint, although beneath this external shell the soft tissues usually decomposed, leaving behind little but the bones. In a few cases the bodily form was skilfully represented by layers of linen bandages and pads of cloth. Great importance seems to have been attached to the outward appearance of the preserved body. The head and limbs were individually wrapped or modelled, and the body was sometimes dressed in garments and provided with jewellery. These Old Kingdom mummies, therefore, closely resembled statues of the individual, representing them as if they were actually alive. In fact at this time both the preserved body and the statue fulfilled the same ritual function, that of acting as a receptacle for the spirit aspect of the deceased.

After the Old Kingdom, techniques of mummification changed and important advances were made. Something approaching a standard method was evolved, and this remained in use for over 2000 years. In the First Intermediate Period (c.2150 BC) the custom arose of wrapping the entire body, including the limbs, in a long bundle, from which only the head emerged, often adorned with a painted mask. This 'classic' mummy shape and the attributes of the mask (gilded or yellow-painted skin, blue-coloured hair) would have been understood by the ancient Egyptians as signs that the dead person had undergone a transformation into a being who possessed divine qualities. In the Middle Kingdom (c.2125–1650 BC) the extraction of the brain – which had perhaps already been performed occasionally in the Old Kingdom – became more widespread, and in the New Kingdom (c.1550–1069 BC) notable advances were made in the preservation of the soft tissues. The success achieved by the embalmers in this respect is illustrated by the strikingly lifelike heads of some of the pharaohs of the 18th and 19th Dynasties, particularly Tuthmosis IV and Sety I. In the Third Intermediate Period (c.1069–664 BC) the skills of the embalmers reached their peak. Special efforts were made to make the body beneath the wrappings appear lifelike, and to achieve this, packing materials were pushed beneath the skin, artificial eyes inserted into the

Fig. 21. *Left:* Unwrapped mummy of a priest of Amun. The chest cavity has been opened to reveal linen-wrapped bundles which contained the preserved internal organs. From Deir el-Bahri, 21st Dynasty, c.1069–945 BC.

sockets and elaborate cosmetic treatments applied to faces, fingernails and hair.

Perhaps to give the dead person full possession of his body, the preserved viscera were now replaced inside the chest and abdomen. From the Late Period to the Roman era (664 BC–AD 395) the emphasis changed once again, with less care expended on the effective preservation of the soft tissues and more attention devoted to the external trappings. Linen wrappings were elaborately arranged in

Fig. 22. *Right:* Unwrapped head of the mummy of a man. Artificial eyes, one of which remains, were inserted into the orbits by the embalmers. Fragments of linen wrappings also survive. CT scanning has shown that the empty skull cavity was stuffed with linen. Third Intermediate Period, c.1069–664 BC. Height 22.5 cm.

Fig. 23. *Left and above:*
Mummy of a woman
named Katebet. X-rays
and CT scans reveal
that the mummification
was rudimentary: the
brain appears to have
been left in the skull,
and the main efforts of
the embalmers were
directed to the outer
wrappings and the
provision of a painted
and gilded mask. From
Thebes. End of the
18th Dynasty, c.1300
BC. Length 1.65 m.

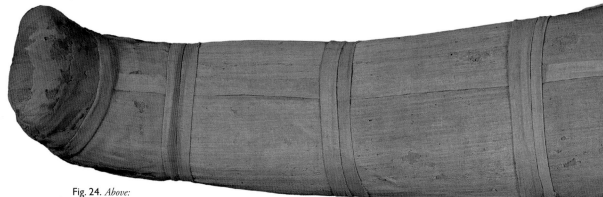

Fig. 24. *Above:* Mummy of a woman named Shepenmehyt. CT scans show that there is a package on the thighs, which probably contains the internal organs. From Thebes. 26th Dynasty, c.600 BC. Length 1.67 m.

Fig. 25. *Below:* CT scan of the head of a mummy, showing linen packing (here coloured purple) which was inserted into the empty skull cavity during embalming. From Thebes, 22nd Dynasty, c.900 BC. Height of mummy 1.69 m.

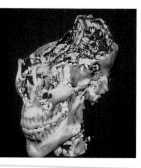

geometrical patterns. During the Late Period, amulets were provided in great profusion between the bandages. In the Ptolemaic and Roman eras faces were adorned with gilded cartonnage masks, painted plaster head-pieces and ultimately images of the dead on wooden panels executed in Classical style, the forerunners of western Renaissance portraiture.

From the third century AD onwards, Egyptian society embraced first Coptic Christianity and then Islam. In these religious environments mummification had no legitimate place. Perhaps influenced by long tradition, the bodies of Coptic monks were sometimes given crude mummification, but the custom was increasingly condemned by the church as a pagan practice and eventually ceased.

How mummies were made

Because of the long history of mummification in Egypt, methods varied at any given period and also changed through time. Herodotus mentions that three different 'grades' of mummification were available, ranging from the basic to the elaborate, with the standard of treatment reflected in the cost. His evidence has been supported by modern examinations of mummies. In the following paragraphs the main steps in mummification at its most effective are described, based on all available sources of information.

The initial stages

The effects of Egypt's hot climate on a corpse would become unpleasantly apparent within a few hours of death. The body would therefore be delivered to the embalmers as soon as possible. Stripped of clothing, it was washed and purged of any decomposition fluids which might have already made their

appearance. The embalmers next set about extracting the internal organs, which would otherwise rot very rapidly and spread irreversible bacterial activity throughout the body. Herodotus stated that this process began with the removal of the brain. The embalmers were immediately presented with a challenge. The head was regarded as a particularly important part of the body, and if it were lost or damaged the deceased's hopes of the afterlife would be threatened. Probably for this reason the embalmers devised a method of extracting the brain which caused minimum damage. The usual technique was to insert a tool into one nostril (generally the left) and to break through the roof of the nasal cavity, giving free access to the cranium. Then a long metal probe, made of iron according to Herodotus, and hooked at one end, was inserted and rotated to break up the brain and to draw it out in pieces via the nostril. Occasionally, the embalmers perforated an eye socket or another part of the skull, such as the

Fig. 26. *Above:* Wax plate bearing the *wedjat* eye. Such plates were placed over the abdominal incision. The eye probably served here to magically 'heal' the embalming wound. New Kingdom, c.1550–1069 BC. Provenance unknown. Length 6.14 cm, width 5.54 cm.

37

Fig. 27.
Above and opposite:
Mummy of an
unidentified man. The
unusual external
appearance of the
mummy is reminiscent
of Old Kingdom
techniques; limbs and
digits were separately
wrapped, the facial
features modelled in
resin-soaked linen
and painted on the
wrappings, and the hair
deliberately left exposed.
From Thebes. After 305
BC. Length 1.62 m.

basal hole (foramen magnum) to extract the brain. The function of the brain was not clearly understood, and the remains seem to have been disposed of. The empty cranium was often filled with linen or sawdust, or molten resin which was poured in through the nasal cavity.

The embalmers next turned their attention to extracting the organs from the chest and abdomen. Herodotus recorded that in the most expensive form of mummification this was done by making an incision in the abdomen, and he was clearly correct: such openings are visible on many mummies. The cut was usually located on the left side of the abdomen, and according to Herodotus it was made with 'a sharp obsidian blade'. The incisions are often found to be quite small and in order to remove the organs the embalmer must have inserted his hand, guiding himself by touch alone. He would first have removed the stomach and intestines and then, after piercing the diaphragm, the lungs and liver. Care was taken to leave the heart in place, as this was believed to be the centre of the person's being, an organ which had an important role to play in his passage to the afterlife (see chapters 3 and 5). The kidneys were sometimes extracted as well, but were more often left in place. The empty cavities of the body were washed out with water and also, according to Herodotus, cleansed with palm wine and spices.

The small size of the abdominal incision in most mummies testifies to the embalmers' efforts to minimize the extent of physical intervention. This probably arose from a notion of the sanctity of the human body, and Diodorus records a tradition that the man who made the incision was cursed and pelted with stones by his colleagues as soon as he had performed his task. This was probably a symbolic act, meant to ward off any undesirable consequences which might follow from performing an operation which was thought to be at once both necessary and improper.

In the cheaper methods of mummification the viscera were not removed via an incision. Herodotus describes how the embalmers injected a corrosive fluid into the rectum using a syringe. He states that this fluid remained in the body until it had dissolved the internal organs, which were then released from the anus as a liquid. Herodotus identifies the substance used as cedar oil (juniper oil is more likely), but this would not have liquefied the viscera in the way he describes and it is possible that he misunderstood the intention of the operation. Mummies have indeed been found which show signs of rectal intervention, but in some of them the viscera remained largely intact, and it may be that the purpose of the fluid was to preserve the organs in situ rather than to dissolve them. This technique was used in the preservation of the bodies of several royal individuals of the 11th Dynasty found at Deir el-Bahri, and also in the embalming of a woman in the Late Period.

The removal of the internal organs would have been performed as quickly as possible, but the next stage in mummification was a lengthy one. It was necessary to dry the corpse thoroughly. By extracting all the liquid the activity of bacteria and bodily enzymes which led to decomposition would be prevented. A simple method of achieving this was to air-dry the body or to bury it in the sand. The latter had accidentally preserved corpses of the Predynastic Period, and sand-drying was sometimes used in pharaonic times to desiccate the bodies of persons of lower status or perhaps those who died in circumstances where more careful treatment was not available. This method seems to have been used, for example, to preserve the remains of sixty soldiers who had been killed in battle, probably during one of the internal conflicts which took place in Egypt during the early Middle Kingdom. They had been buried together in a tomb at Deir el-Bahri, but apart from a rapid drying with sand and wrapping in linen, they had not received any other formal treatment. On many of them the wounds of which they had died were visible and parts of arrows were still embedded in some of the bodies.

However, in the most elaborate method of mummification the drying agent was a compound of sodium salts which occurs naturally in Egypt. This substance is called natron, a term which derives from the ancient Egyptian word *netjery*, 'divine [salt]' – a reflection of its special qualities as a preservative and purifying agent. Natron is found at several locations in Egypt, notably at El-Kab and in the Wadi Natrun in the Libyan Desert, once a branch of the Nile and now a series of salt lakes. The substance is found as a dry deposit on the lake beds and around their shores. The property which most distinguished natron as a preservative was its ability to absorb moisture, but it may also have played a part in breaking down the body's fats, which would otherwise liquefy and contribute to its decay. Numerous samples of Egyptian embalming salts have been analysed in the laboratory, and these tests have shown that the principal constituents were sodium carbonate and sodium bicarbonate, but sodium chloride and sodium sulphate were usually present as well. The proportions of these constituents varied; some ancient samples have turned out to consist almost entirely of sodium chloride (common salt). This may be because the natural deposits of inorganic salts which the Egyptians exploited varied in chemical composition.

The manner of use of the salt is not described in detail in ancient writings. Herodotus states simply that the embalmers covered the corpse with natron. In the nineteenth century a misunderstanding of this passage led to a belief that the bodies were soaked in a solution of natron, but although natron in solution has been found in a few tombs the bulk of the evidence indicates that the salt was usually employed in a dry form. Loose natron was heaped over the body, and the chest and abdominal cavities were packed with natron in small linen packages.

Fig. 28.
Opposite and above:
Mummy of an adolescent boy. X rays and CT scans show that the skeleton was in disorder when the body was wrapped. The face is covered by an encaustic portrait of the boy painted on a wooden panel. These panels were typical of the Roman Period, as was the layered arrangement of the outer wrappings. The gilded cartonnage footcase depicts the feet wearing sandals. From Hawara. AD 100–120. Length 1.33 m.

41

Fig. 29.
Above and opposite:
The mummy of
Cleopatra, a 17-year-
old girl, daughter of
Soter. CT scans
revealed that the chest
cavity contains three
unidentified bundles
and that the body was
densely packed,
perhaps with sand or
mud. It is wrapped in
many layers of linen
with an outer shroud
bearing a painted
representation of the
dead woman in the
image of the goddess
Hathor. From Thebes.
Early second century
AD. Length 1.68 m.

These packages have often been found inside mummies and among the detritus left over after mummification. Modern experimentation using rats and birds has demonstrated that natron is most effective as a preservative when in dry form. Textual sources indicate that approximately 35 days were required to thoroughly dry a body. The quantity of natron used is nowhere recorded, but in a modern experiment an adult human body was mummified according to ancient Egyptian methodology, with dry natron as the desiccant. The investigators found that more than 270 kg of natron was required to dry the body, which itself weighed 85 kg. The dehydration process reduced the body to almost half of its original weight.

Rebuilding the body

At the end of the drying period the embalmers removed the natron from the corpse. Most of the fatty tissues would have broken down and the skin would have become loose and wrinkled. The drying process may also have contributed to the dark discolouration of the skin which is seen on many mummies. The body had, however, been purged of all the products of corruption, one of the chief aims of mummification according to Egyptian notions, but this purification was only part of the process. The corpse had now to be 'rebuilt' and transformed into a new kind of body, one in which the corrupt substances were replaced with materials of magical and divine significance.

First the body cavities were washed to remove any traces of natron, and then the spaces were filled with packing materials – often rolls of linen, sawdust and earth; sometimes dried lichen was used. The body was also treated with beeswax, plant oils and animal fats, which inhibited decay caused by microbial activity. These substances were poured into the body cavities and rubbed into the skin, helping also to lend suppleness to the dried-out limbs and to produce a pleasant smell. According to the *Ritual of Embalming,* one purpose of the anointing was to give the deceased the 'odour of a god'. Religious associations also determined some of the substances that were used in this way. Besides various imported coniferous resins, such as cedar oil, the Egyptians frequently used pistacia resin, from which they also made incense. Their word for incense, *senetjer,* means 'that which makes divine', and when applied to a mummy it apparently conferred divine status on the deceased. Bitumen was sometimes applied and came into more widespread use in mummification during the later centuries of the pharaonic era, even giving rise to the word 'mummy' (see pages 9 and 142). However, the extent of its use remains uncertain, because without chemical analysis it is impossible to distinguish bitumen from the various plant oils and resins which the embalmers used regularly.

Fig. 30. *Right:* Plates made of gold leaf to cover the eye and tongue of a mummy. Roman Period, after 30 BC. Length of eye 2.9 cm; length of tongue 4.5 cm.

The embalmers also made efforts to beautify the shrunken corpse and to restore it to a more lifelike appearance by arranging the hair and applying cosmetics. The most elaborate treatments were made in the 21st Dynasty (*c.*1069–945 BC), when the art of mummification in Egypt reached its peak. To fill out the shrivelled features and limbs the embalmers made a series of incisions in the skin. Using small probes, they introduced packing materials under the skin and smoothed out the surfaces to give a plumper, more naturalistic appearance. Mud, linen, sawdust and sand were all used for this process. Some packing was inserted through the abdominal incision which had been made to extract the viscera, and then carefully pushed into place to fill the neck, the chest, the back and the upper parts of the legs. The upper limbs were packed via incisions in the shoulders. Special care was taken to restore the features of the face, and to do this packing was inserted through the mouth into the cheeks. The faces of some mummies of the 21st Dynasty have a bloated appearance caused by the over-use of stuffing, and in the case of Henuttawy, wife of the high priest of Amun Pinedjem I, so much packing was inserted that the cheeks burst open.

A further measure to create an appearance of life was adopted in the 21st and 22nd Dynasties, through the use of artificial eyes made of stone or coloured glass. The actual eyes were usually left *in situ* by the embalmers but the drying process caused them to shrink, so replicas were placed in the sockets, and the eyelids were raised to give the impression that the person was both alive and wakeful. Care was taken to prevent the loss of the nails through the loosening of the skin, and in the most elaborate burials finger- and toe-stalls of gold and silver were fitted before the body was wrapped.

A few mummies have been found in which part of the body is missing and has been replaced by a prosthesis. In two cases this was a big toe which had evidently been lost through injury or disease, and the replacement appears to have been made to be worn during life and then to have been kept with the body during

Fig. 31. *Left:*
Painted sandstone statue
of Amenhotep I. The
double crown of Upper
and Lower Egypt denotes
the ruler's status. His
body is shrouded in a
white linen garment,
which signifies that he is
undergoing regeneration
like the god Osiris, who
was depicted in a similar
manner. From Deir el-
Bahri, 18th Dynasty,
c.1510 BC. Height 2.69 m.

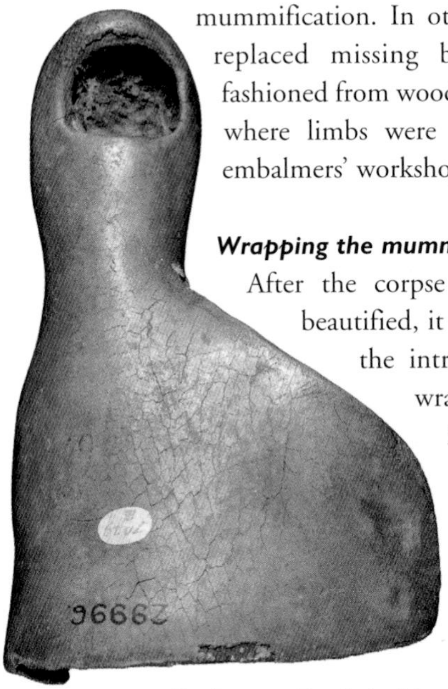

Fig. 32. *Right:*
A prosthetic toe,
made of cartonnage
and painted to match
the wearer's skin.
Holes along the edges
suggest it was worn in
life and attached to a
sandal or shoe. It was
replaced on the body
after mummification.
From Thebes. Probably
Third Intermediate
Period, c.1069–664 BC.
Length 11.9 cm.

Fig. 33. *Opposite:*
Cartonnage mummy-
mask of a woman
named Satdjehuty. The
blue colouring of the
hair and the gold leaf
on the face symbolized
the divine status which
the dead were thought
to attain. Sheets of fine
linen which belonged
to the mask's owner
bear inscriptions in ink
stating that she was a
favoured courtier of
Ahmose-Nefertary, the
wife of King Ahmose I.
From Thebes. Early
18th Dynasty, c.1500
BC. Height 52 cm.

mummification. In other cases the embalmers seem to have replaced missing body parts with substitutes crudely fashioned from wood or linen. These may represent instances where limbs were lost at the time of death or in the embalmers' workshop.

Wrapping the mummy

After the corpse had been fully dried, anointed and beautified, it was wrapped. At an early period, before the introduction of artificial preservation, the wrappings helped to retain the physical integrity of the corpse, which might otherwise fall apart or be scattered by scavenging animals. Later the wrappings acquired a symbolic significance, particularly from the First Intermediate Period onward, when the canonical image of the mummy with limbs confined inside a shroud came into fashion. A body enveloped in a tight-fitting shroud or garment was supposed to be in a transitional state of being, one which would lead to renewed life. The shrouded royal statues, which were a feature of many temples, depicted the king in this state of potential rebirth, which was made possible by the life-giving power of the god who dwelt in the temple. Although these sculptural images resemble Osiris (and are often called 'Osiride statues' in consequence), they were not directly linked with that deity. Osiris, the statues and the mummified bodies of the dead all shared the same appearance because the enveloping wrappings denoted that they were endowed with the capacity to be regenerated.

Because of the religious significance of wrapping, this part of the mummification process was carried out in a strongly ritualized context. The wrappings were usually of linen, and texts explain that they were supposedly made by Tayet, goddess of weaving, or by the weavers of the goddess Neith. Royal mummies were wrapped in special linen, sometimes cloths which had been previously used in temple rituals, but humbler people made do with old clothes and bedsheets which were recycled as shrouds or torn into strips as bandages. The usual method was first to wrap the head and the limbs separately, and then to apply several layers of cloth around the whole body. Some of the layers would be soaked in oils or molten resin. Large sheets alternated with layers of narrow strips wound around the mummy. Sometimes huge quantities of cloth were used: the

mummy of the Theban official Wah (late 11th Dynasty) was cocooned in over 375 square metres of linen. In its completed state, Wah's mummy was a massive, amorphous bundle, from which the head, covered by a mask, protruded. However, the embalmers usually aimed to create a mummy which reproduced the main contours of the human form, including the shoulders and feet. To achieve this, they carefully positioned folded sheets, rolls and bundles of cloth between the layers as the wrapping proceeded. This must have necessitated frequent lifting and turning of the body as more and more layers were put on, and this manipulation occasionally led to mistakes. One 18th Dynasty mummy found undisturbed in a tomb at Thebes was lying face-down in his coffin. While wrapping him, the embalmers had apparently forgotten which was the front and which the back. To fashion the prescribed shape they had placed a bundle of cloth under the outer shroud in the position where they assumed the feet must be – but they had guessed wrongly, and had completed the wrappings with the body turned around.

The *Ritual of Embalming* specifies the positioning of particular pieces of cloth, with details of their shape, colour and exact location. Special incantations were to be spoken as each piece was applied. Some of the cloths were associated with deities, such as Hathor, Thoth and Re-Horakhty. The *Ritual* describes the correct application of these and also provides instructions for the placing of amulets between the layers of wrappings (see chapter 3). In the most elaborate mummification, when all these directions were observed with strict accuracy, the wrapping could occupy up to thirty days, but for those who paid only for a simpler procedure a few days probably sufficed.

Fig. 34. *Above:* Gilded cartonnage mummy-mask. Around the head words from spell 151 of the *Book of the Dead* identify the dead person's bodily parts with those of various gods and goddesses. Provenance unknown. Late Ptolemaic Period, first century BC. Height 44 cm.

Fig. 35. *Opposite:* Mask from the mummy of a woman named Aphrodite. An inscription records that she died at the age of twenty. From Hawara. AD 50–70. Height 53.5 cm.

Fig. 36. *Right:* Painted plaster mask. These plaster heads were cast in moulds as an alternative to portrait panels on mummies of the Roman Period. The eyes are separately made, of glass. The woman is depicted wearing earrings and beads, the forms of which, together with the hairstyle, point to a date around the end of the first century AD. Provenance unknown. Height 33.3 cm, width 30 cm.

Masks: seeing 'with the head of a god'

In many periods the mummy was not considered complete until a mask had been placed over the face. The mask played an important part in the transformation of the body which mummification was supposed to promote. Though they are often wrongly described as 'death masks', the mummy headpieces did not reflect the true appearance of the wearer either during life or at the time of death. Rather they represented them in the transfigured state which they aspired to reach, and so the faces are idealized, showing the person physically perfect and eternally young. On the finer examples the exposed face is covered with gold leaf, a sign

APTEMIΔWPE·EYΨYXI

Fig. 37. *Left and above:*
Mummy of a young man
named Artemidorus,
enclosed within a stucco
case, with pharaonic
funerary scenes in gold
leaf. These include Anubis
tending the mummy on
a lion-bier, the fetish of
Abydos flanked by Horus
and Thoth, and Osiris
awakening to new life.
An encaustic portrait
set into the case depicts
Artemidorus wearing a
wreath. From Hawara. AD
100–120. Height 1.71 m.

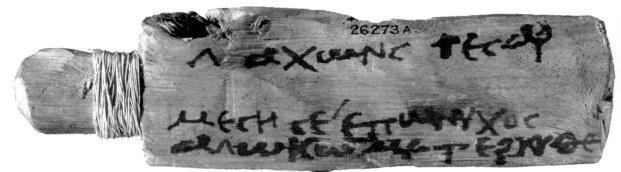

Fig. 38. *Above:* Wooden mummy label from a male mummy found at Deir el-Bahri. The Greek inscription names the deceased as Pakhons, son of Mesesis, grandson of Eponuchos, from the village of Terkythis. For the painted mummy-cover, see page 103. 3rd century AD. Length 16.4 cm.

that the wearer had become divine, since the gods are described in inscriptions as having flesh of gold.

The concept of fashioning an idealized face for the deceased had a long history in Egypt. Clay masks have been found in graves of the late Predynastic Period at Hierakonpolis, and these were probably placed on the bodies of the dead. In elite mummification in the Old Kingdom the face was sometimes coated with liquid plaster or resin-soaked linen, in which the features were carefully modelled. It was not until the First Intermediate Period that the helmet-like mask became common. These masks were usually made from cartonnage (a lightweight fabric formed from layers of linen soaked in animal glue and coated with plaster). They enveloped the head completely and usually depict the deceased wearing a wig, headband and bead-collar. Some masks were inscribed with a spell found in the *Coffin Texts* and later in the *Book of the Dead,* which goes a long way to explain the mask's function. It is there called the 'head of mystery', or 'mysterious head', and its main functions were to enable the wearer to see in the afterlife and to drive away any enemies or hostile forces which might attack him. The deceased person is described as seeing 'with the head of a god'. He is therefore able to act as a deity, and to emphasize this divine status the spell also enumerates the main parts of the head, equating each of them with a corresponding member of a god's body: 'The crown of your head is that of Anubis, the back of your head is that of Horus …'

The internal organs

In the most expensive method of mummification, all the internal organs with the exception of the heart were removed. The brain was disposed of, as were often the kidneys. The liver, lungs, stomach and intestines were set aside for preservation. Diodorus records that they were cleansed with palm wine and spices, which is possible but cannot be confirmed. Evidence from the examination of actual mummified viscera indicates that they were usually preserved in a similar manner to the body itself, by drying with natron, coating with resin and wrapping in linen. The organs were made into packages, usually four in number. Each organ package could be regarded as a separate embodiment of the deceased and in burials of persons of high status the bundles were placed in individual anthropoid coffins, like miniature mummies. The more usual method, however, was to store them in rectangular chests or in sets of four jars which had lids in the form of human or animal heads. These vessels are known to Egyptologists as 'canopic jars' (see page 54).

The canopic jars were placed in the tomb, usually close to the foot of the coffin. They were often enclosed within a cubic chest of stone or wood. A second level of protection for the viscera was provided by four goddesses – Isis, Nephthys, Neith and Selkis – who were often depicted on the sides or corners of the chest. Inscriptions mention their tutelary role and explain that they gave protection to the Sons of Horus who, in turn, guarded the body parts assigned to them.

Fig. 39. *Below:* Set of canopic jars which contained the embalmed internal organs of Gua, physician to the governor of the Hare-province. The jars are of calcite with human-headed lids of painted wood. They were stored in the tomb in the wooden chest inscribed with Gua's name and title. From Deir el-Bersha. 12th Dynasty, c.1870 BC. Height of chest 53 cm.

CANOPIC JARS

Fig. 40. *Below:* Canopic jars of Neskhons, wife of the high priest of Amun Pinedjem II. Made of wood and calcite. From Deir el-Bahri. 21st Dynasty, c.970 BC. Heights 36.5 to 40 cm.

The main internal organs of the body which the embalmers attempted to preserve were placed inside four jars. The lids of these containers (at least from the New Kingdom onwards) represented the heads of four minor deities, the Sons of Horus. One organ was entrusted to the care of each of these gods. Imsety, with a human head, guarded the liver. Baboon-headed Hapy protected the lungs. Jackal-headed Duamutef watched over the stomach, and falcon-headed Qebehsenuef was responsible for the intestines.

Though now known as 'canopic jars,' this was not their ancient name. In the Delta town of Canopus there was reputed to be a cult in which the object of veneration was an image shaped like a vase with a human head. This was probably a local form of the god Osiris, but Classical writers linked both town and vase-fetish with Canopus, the legendary pilot of Menelaus, who was supposed to have been buried near that spot. Although there is no connection with the vessels used to hold mummified viscera, the term 'canopic' has now become firmly attached both to these jars and to the chests that contained them.

59197

59198

In the Third Intermediate Period the treatment of the preserved viscera changed. Each bundle now contained an organ accompanied by a figurine of one of the four sons of Horus, made of wax or a mixture of wax and resin. The packages were replaced in the chest cavity before the mummy was wrapped. Canopic jars therefore had no practical purpose, but out of respect for tradition they continued to be placed in the tomb. Some of these were genuine jars, left empty; others were imitations carved from solid pieces of stone or wood to resemble canopic jars. In the Late Period the use of the jars was revived, but not universally; in many burials the preserved viscera were placed inside the mummy wrappings between the legs.

The embalmers

Mummification was carried out in the vicinity of the tombs, probably close to the Nile or to some other water-source such as a canal. Most of the operations seem to have been performed in temporary structures such as tents or booths made of reeds and matting. Sometimes mud brick buildings may have been used, and remains of such structures have been found outside some tombs. The preliminary washing of the corpse took place in the *ibu*, or *ibu en wab*, 'tent of purification'. For royal burials in the Old Kingdom a structure called the *seh-netjer* ('divine booth') was used for this purpose. The body was then taken to the embalmers workshop where the most lengthy portion of the operation, involving evisceration, desiccation and wrapping, took place. This was called the *wabet* ('pure place' or 'place of purification') or *per-nefer* ('house of rejuvenation').

The actual personnel who carried out the mummification were organized into a hierarchy. In charge of the operations was an official called the *hery seshta,* or 'Master of Secrets'. He was closely associated with the god Anubis, who was supposed to have mummified Osiris. Other officials involved were the 'God's seal-bearer' and the *khery-hebet,* the 'lector priest', who recited the appropriate ritual incantations as the operation proceeded. Below these men in rank was the *wet,* the embalmer proper, who performed the practical parts of the process – washing, eviscerating, drying, applying oils and spices, packing and wrapping. Egyptian texts do not distinguish

Fig. 41. *Opposite:* Demotic contract, stipulating who would be responsible for mummifying the dead at a cemetery at Asyut, and what materials were to be used. 157 BC Height 31 cm.

Fig. 42. *Below:* Beeswax figures of the four Sons of Horus. During the Third Intermediate Period, these were placed inside the body cavity before the mummy was wrapped. 21st to 25th Dynasties, c.1069–664 BC. Heights 13.3 cm.

between the embalmers who carried out these various tasks, but in Greek sources two specialists are mentioned, the *paraschistes,* or 'incision maker', and the *taricheutes.* The latter (which literally means 'pickler') had the task of drying the body.

Documents surviving from the Ptolemaic and Roman periods reveal that embalmers belonged to a highly organized profession. When a person died, the relatives would make a legal contract with the local embalmers, who agreed to perform their work by a specified day and to return the corpse to the family at that time. A number of these documents survive on papyrus, and include receipts for some of the materials which the embalmers used in preserving the body. Mummification, however, was not always carried out by professionals. Sometimes it might be done by a work colleague; registers of attendance by the royal tomb builders of Deir el-Medina occasionally mention such things. In year 40 of the reign of Ramesses II, Amenemwia was absent from work because he was 'mummifying Hormose'.

Proper procedure was not always followed, even by the professional embalmers. There are numerous examples of careless treatment of bodies. Some mummies,

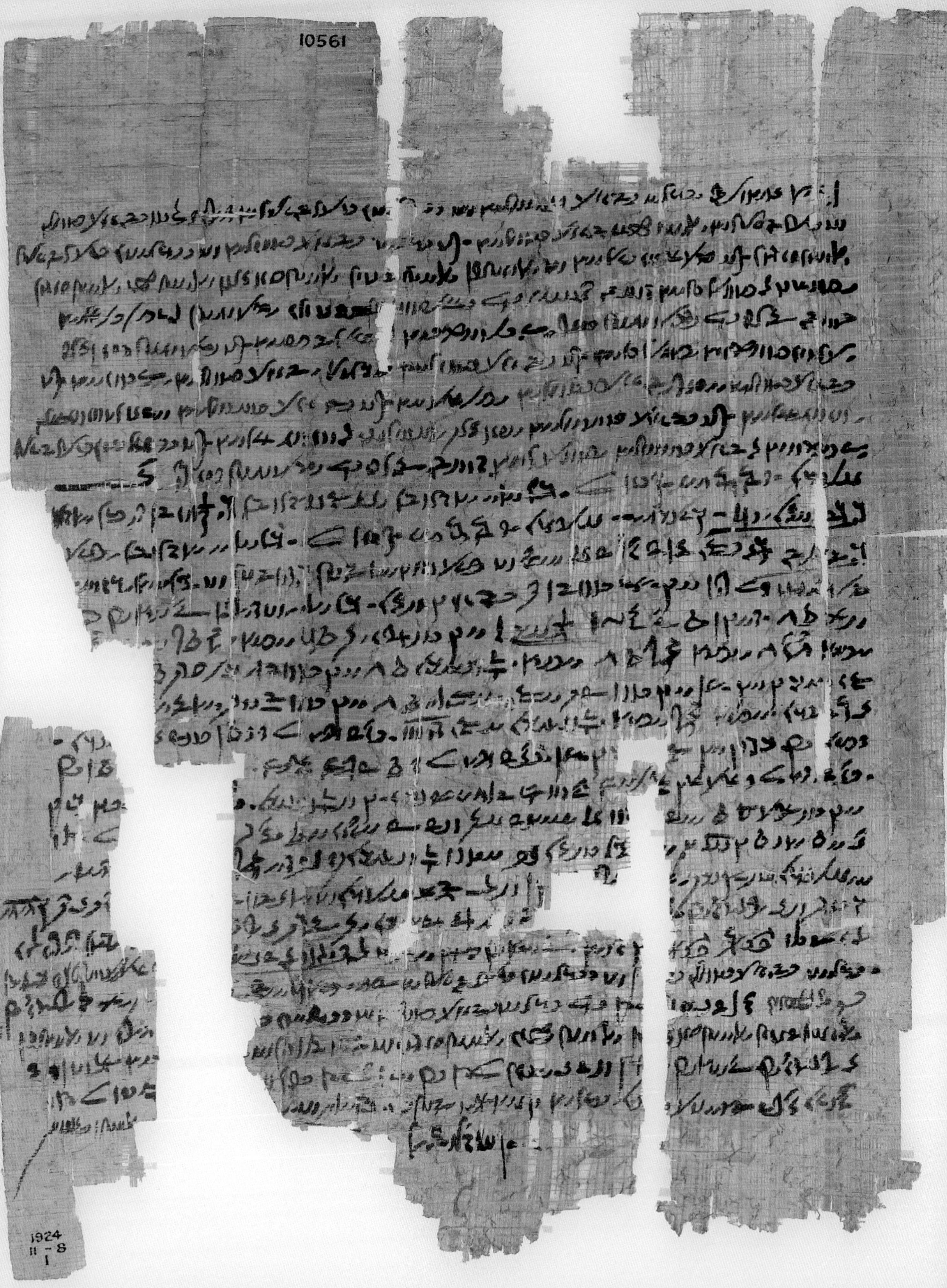
10561
1924
II-8
I

Fig. 43. *Right:* Cartonnage case containing the mummy of the priest of Khons, Nesperennub. Thebes, 22nd Dynasty, *c.*800 BC. Height 1.73 m.

which appear perfect externally, have been found on unwrapping or x-raying to contain a badly damaged or incomplete body. Sometimes mistakes by the embalmers were concealed within the wrappings. Beneath the bandages of the Theban priest Nesperennub (*c.*800 BC) a crude clay bowl was detected by CT scans, stuck to the back of the head (fig. 44, page 59). It had apparently been used to catch drips of molten resin during the embalming and had become firmly glued to the skull. Around one hundred years later, another Theban official, Padiamenet, was also mummified in an unconventional manner. The head became loose and the embalmers joined it back to the body with a wooden pole. They were also unable to fit the mummy inside the cartonnage case which had been prepared for it, and left the feet protruding from the bottom. During the wrapping process insects and animals often crept between layers of bandages and sometimes became unintended companions for the deceased on the journey to the afterlife. A mouse and a lizard were found between the wrappings of the 11th Dynasty mummy of Wah, mentioned on page 49. In spite of such mistakes, embalmers were generally treated with honour and respect, according to Diodorus, although Herodotus' account is more negative. He paints a picture of them as untrustworthy, and even records a story that the corpses of young women and wives of high-ranking men were only handed over for mummification on the third or fourth day after death to prevent the embalmers from committing acts of necrophilia.

Although the embalming and wrapping of corpses was a crucial stage in the passage to eternity, the mummy was not the final form which the deceased would occupy in the afterlife. The linen wrappings which enclosed the body had an ambivalent role: they

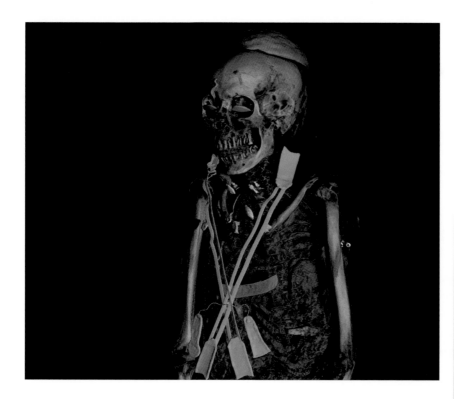

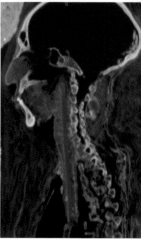

Fig. 44. *Left:*
CT scan of the mummy
of Nesperennub (see
fig. 43, opposite),
showing amulets and
leather bands in situ
beneath the bandages,
and a pottery bowl
which had become
stuck to the head
during the embalming
process. Thebes, 22nd
Dynasty, c.800 BC.

prevented the disintegration of the corpse and the scattering of the bodily members, but they also restricted the limbs, denying the possibility of movement. The Egyptians hoped ultimately to be released from these confining bandages, so that they might enjoy the use of their limbs and be able to dress in garments like those worn by the living. Funerary texts often speak of throwing off the wrappings in the next world. Hence the mummy was a transitional state, a kind of cocoon, from which a new person was to emerge.

Fig. 45. *Above:*
CT scan of the mummy
of Padiamenet, showing
a wooden pole which
the embalmers used to
secure the head to the
body. Thebes, 25th
Dynasty, c.725 BC.

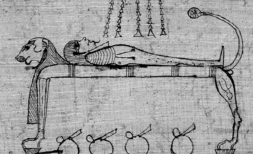

CHAPTER 3

ADORNMENT AND MAGICAL PROTECTION

AT ALL LEVELS OF EGYPTIAN SOCIETY it was the custom to place jewellery and amulets on the bodies of the dead. Items of jewellery, besides adorning the deceased, were indications of status and also carried symbolic or magical significance, providing the wearer with divine protection and special powers. Amulets fulfilled this last requirement even more specifically.

Some of the items of jewellery which were placed on the body had been worn during the owner's lifetime. Tutankhamun's mummy was loaded with rings, bracelets, collars and pectoral ornaments, and further examples were stored in boxes in his tomb. This rich provision of jewellery was probably typical for royal burials. Very few examples from other tombs have survived into modern times, but among those that did were the mummy trappings of three wives of Tuthmosis III (c.1479–1425 BC), which included elaborate golden headdresses, as well as rings, bracelets and collars. Courtiers and officials probably took their jewellery into the afterlife to serve as status symbols, reflections of their rank in the earthly life which they wished to retain after death. General Djehuty, an army commander in the reign of Tuthmosis III, about whose adventures a story survives on a papyrus, was rewarded by his king with many objects of gold which he took with him into his tomb at Saqqara. His mummy was discovered in the early 19th century, and the treasure dispersed, finding its way to several European museums. One piece, now in the British Museum, is a massive gold ring with a rectangular bezel, incised with the name of Djehuty's royal master. These rare survivals make absolutely clear the temptation which elite tombs presented to thieves. Because the most valuable objects were usually placed on the body itself, robbers, working in haste and secrecy, often tore the mummy apart to retrieve jewellery more easily and burnt the coffins to separate their gold coverings from the wood. Many mummies were destroyed in this way. A papyrus recording the trial of a group of Theban tomb robbers, which took place about 1110 BC, includes a remarkable confession by one of them, the stonemason Amenpanefer, in which he describes how he and his gang rifled the burial of King Sebekemsaf II (c.1590 BC) and his wife: 'A great number of *wedjat*-eyes (see pages 70–2) and ornaments of gold were at his neck; his head covering was of gold. The noble mummy of this king was entirely overlaid with gold; his coffins were bedecked with gold, inside and out, inlaid with every kind of precious stone. We collected together the gold which we found on the noble

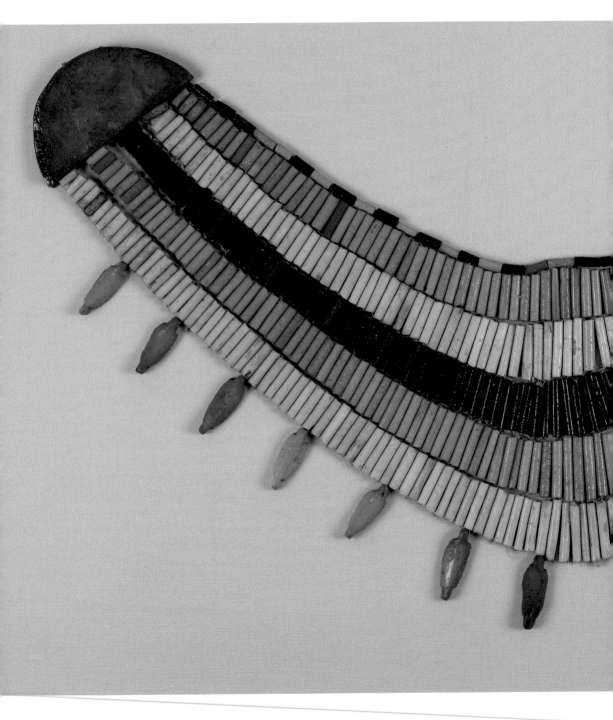

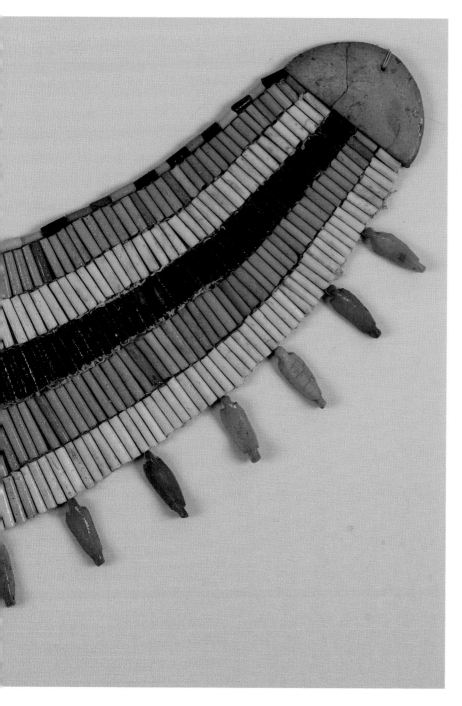

Fig. 49. *Left:*
Broad collar (*wesekh*)
of tubular faience
beads with an outer
row of pendants. It
was found in the tomb
of a female member
of the court of King
Mentuhotep II. Deir
el-Bahri, tomb 4. 11th
Dynasty, c.2020 BC.
Length 54.3 cm.

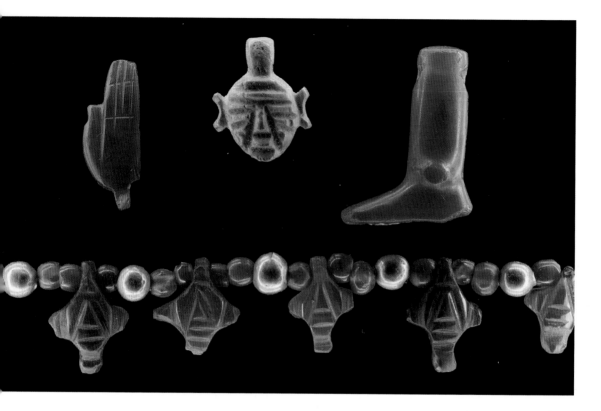

Fig. 50. *Above:* Early specimens of amulets, in the form of a human hand, face and leg, and a series of face-amulets strung on a necklace. Carnelian, bone and gold. 6th–10th Dynasties, c.2300–2025 BC. Heights: 1.8 cm (hand), 1.4 cm (face), 2.2 cm (leg). Length of necklace, 24.8 cm.

mummy of this god and his *wedjat*-eyes and ornaments at his neck [and] the coffins in which he rested. We found the queen likewise; we collected together all that we found on her also. We set fire to their coffins.'

A proportion of the jewellery placed on the mummy was not worn in life but prepared specifically for the tomb. These funerary items were often made in prescribed forms, or incorporated amuletic motifs to give protection and special powers to the wearer. Collars were particularly important in this respect. The *wesekh* ('broad') collar was distinguished by its often having terminals in the shape of falcon-heads; it is a type which is very often depicted on mummy masks and anthropoid coffins. Collars in other shapes were also provided, and spells in the *Book of the Dead* give descriptions of them with precise instructions for the manner in which they were to be placed on the body. Chapter 157 was the 'spell for the vulture of gold placed at the throat of the deceased', and a golden collar of this form, inlaid with coloured glass, was actually found on the mummy of Tutankhamun. The appropriate spell explains that the vulture in this instance represented the goddess Isis extending her protective wings around the dead person, just as she was supposed to have guarded her son Horus. For such collars and other items to function properly, it was important that the correct ritual should be observed when they were placed on the mummy. So chapter 157 ends with a note to guide the priest who would be responsible: 'to be spoken over a vulture of gold, inscribed with this spell, and given as a magical protection to the deceased on the day of burial.'

In many cases this amuletic jewellery could not really have been worn. Some of the collars have no perforations for the attachment of the strings which would secure them to the neck; others lack the counterpoise which hung at the back to prevent the collar from slipping out of place. Some bracelets were too small to envelop the wrists and therefore could not have been fastened. Some of these items were made of precious materials, but others were of flimsy construction, serving only as imitations of the genuine article. But like dummy canopic jars (see pages 53–54), they would perform their functions by magic just as well as real examples; all that was necessary was that they should be placed between the wrappings of the mummy to the accompaniment of the prescribed rituals.

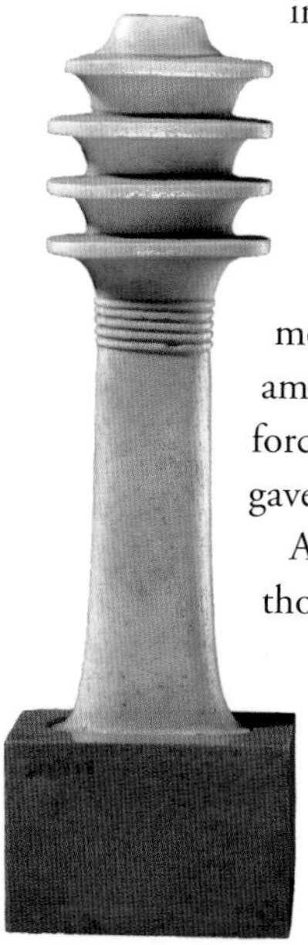

Fig. 51. *Left:* *Tit* amulet, a representation of a girdle or sash looped and tied in the middle. Its function, to give the protection of Isis, is stated in *Book of the Dead* spell 156. There the amulet is prescribed to be made of red jasper, as this example is. The colour denotes the blood of the goddess. It bears a crude inscription giving the name of the owner, Nefer. 19th or 20th Dynasty, c.1250–1100 BC. Height 6.5 cm.

Even more numerous than the items of jewellery were the individual amulets which were placed within the mummy's wrappings. As was the case with funerary jewellery it was often thought necessary for an incantation to be spoken over the amulet to make it effective; the words of some of these spells are included in the *Book of the Dead*. Amulets were often used by the living as a protection against disease or to assist the mother and baby through the hazards of childbirth. Funerary amulets protected the integrity of the corpse, warded off harmful forces, endowed the owner with possessions for the afterlife, and gave him special powers – particularly those of different deities.

Amulets were used in Egypt for over three millennia and many thousands of specimens have come to light. Small lapis lazuli amulets in the form of animals have been found in elite burials at Abydos dating from the very beginning of the First Dynasty (*c.*3000 BC). Another early category of amulets represented parts of the human body, such as the hand, foot or face, perhaps to ensure that the wearer would retain the use of these members even if the body were injured. Amulets of

Fig. 52. *Left:* Faience *djed* pillar amulet, a symbolic representation of the backbone of the god Osiris. Spell 155 of the *Book of the Dead* activated this amulet when placed on the mummy's throat. Late Period, c.600–300 BC. Height 9.4 cm.

AMULETS

Fig. 53. *Below (detail):*
Four spells from the
Book of the Dead with
depictions of amulets and
the texts which activated
them. Left to right: spell
155 (*djed* pillar), spell 156
(*tit*, or Isis-knot), spell
29B (heart amulet) and
spell 166 (headrest
amulet). Papyrus of Ani,
Thebes. 19th Dynasty,
c.1275 BC. Height 42 cm.

In essence, an amulet was a small object which served as a medium to endow its owner with supernatural powers or qualities. Some amulets were natural in origin, such as shells, but the majority were carved or moulded from stone, semi-precious stone, metal, faience, glass, ceramic or wood. Their power was believed to reside in their shape, their colour, and the material from which they were made. Gold was especially valued because it was supposed to confer divine status and eternal life, while the colour green was associated with plants and, by extension, with the idea of the renewal of life.

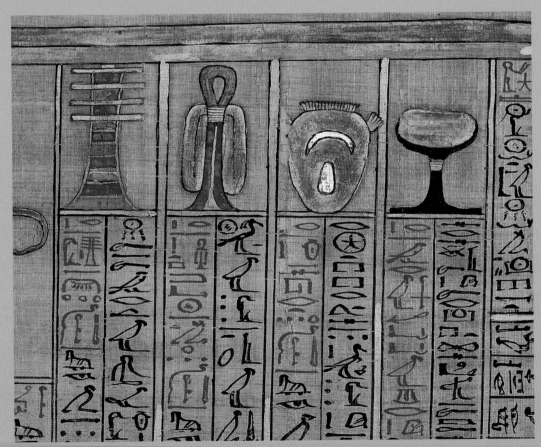

this type are chiefly found in graves of the First Intermediate Period (*c.*2100 BC), but in later centuries they fell out of use, possibly because advances in mummification reduced the need for such safeguards.

During the New Kingdom, the range of amulets provided for the dead was still fairly limited. A very common one was the *djed,* which resembles a pillar or column with four bars arranged horizontally across the top (see fig. 52, page 67). The image may have been derived from a tree trunk with its branches cut off, for the object played a part in a very ancient ritual, the 'Raising of the *djed*', where the pillar was pulled into an upright position by the use of ropes. It was originally associated with the gods Sokar and Ptah, but came to be regarded as a symbol of Osiris. Because the pillar bore a resemblance to a human spine, the *djed* was later reinterpreted as the backbone of Osiris. Chapter 155 of the *Book of the Dead* emphasizes this link, part of the text declaring: 'Raise yourself up, Osiris! You have your backbone once more, O weary-hearted one; you have your vertebrae.' The *djed* pillar therefore endowed the deceased with endurance and the capacity to stand upright. Amulets in this shape were produced in large numbers. The *Book of the Dead* recommended that the *djed* should be placed on the throat, and

Fig. 54. *Left:*
Wedjat amulet of haematite, representing the eye of the god Horus, which was believed to have been injured and subsequently healed. It signified 'wholeness' and conferred protection on its owner. The markings beneath the eye are based on those of a falcon, the form in which Horus was often depicted. Late Period, *c.*600-300 BC. Length 2.4 cm.

Fig. 55. *Below:* Faience amulets representing deities, whose powers and protection would be transferred to the owner. Left to right: Isis, Nephthys, Anubis, Horus, Thoth. Late Period, 600–300 BC. Heights 3.6–4.1 cm.

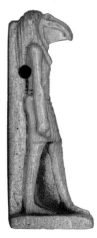

Fig. 56. *Above:* Faience pectoral in the shape of a shrine or pylon with a cornice. It incorporates a large heart-scarab inscribed with spell 30B of the *Book of the Dead* on behalf of a woman called Ptahemheb. The scarab is depicted in the solar barque receiving the adoration of the goddesses Isis and Nephthys. *Wedjat* eyes and *djed* and *tit* emblems are also included in the scene. Probably from the Memphite necropolis, 19th Dynasty. Height 9.7 cm.

indeed many examples have been found at this spot on mummies. At first only one *djed* was provided, but in tombs of the Late Period it is not uncommon to find ten or more on a single mummy.

Closely related to the *djed* pillar was the *tit*-amulet, which represented a loop of cloth tied as a girdle. It was associated with the goddess Isis, wife of Osiris, and – according to chapter 156 of the *Book of the Dead* – a *tit* amulet made of red jasper placed on the mummy's throat would provide the power of Isis to protect the dead person. The *djed* and *tit* appear frequently in tombs, and not only as amulets; they are also seen painted on coffins, on the walls of tomb chapels, and as friezes on chests and shrines. In the 21st Dynasty anthropoid coffins often hold a wooden *djed* and a *tit* in their crossed hands (see fig. 67, page 88).

Perhaps the commonest of all amulets placed on mummies was the eye of Horus, or *wedjat*. This takes the form of the eye of a falcon with its distinctive facial markings. The two eyes of the god Horus the Elder were supposed to be the sun and the moon. Horus was continually in conflict against the god Seth,

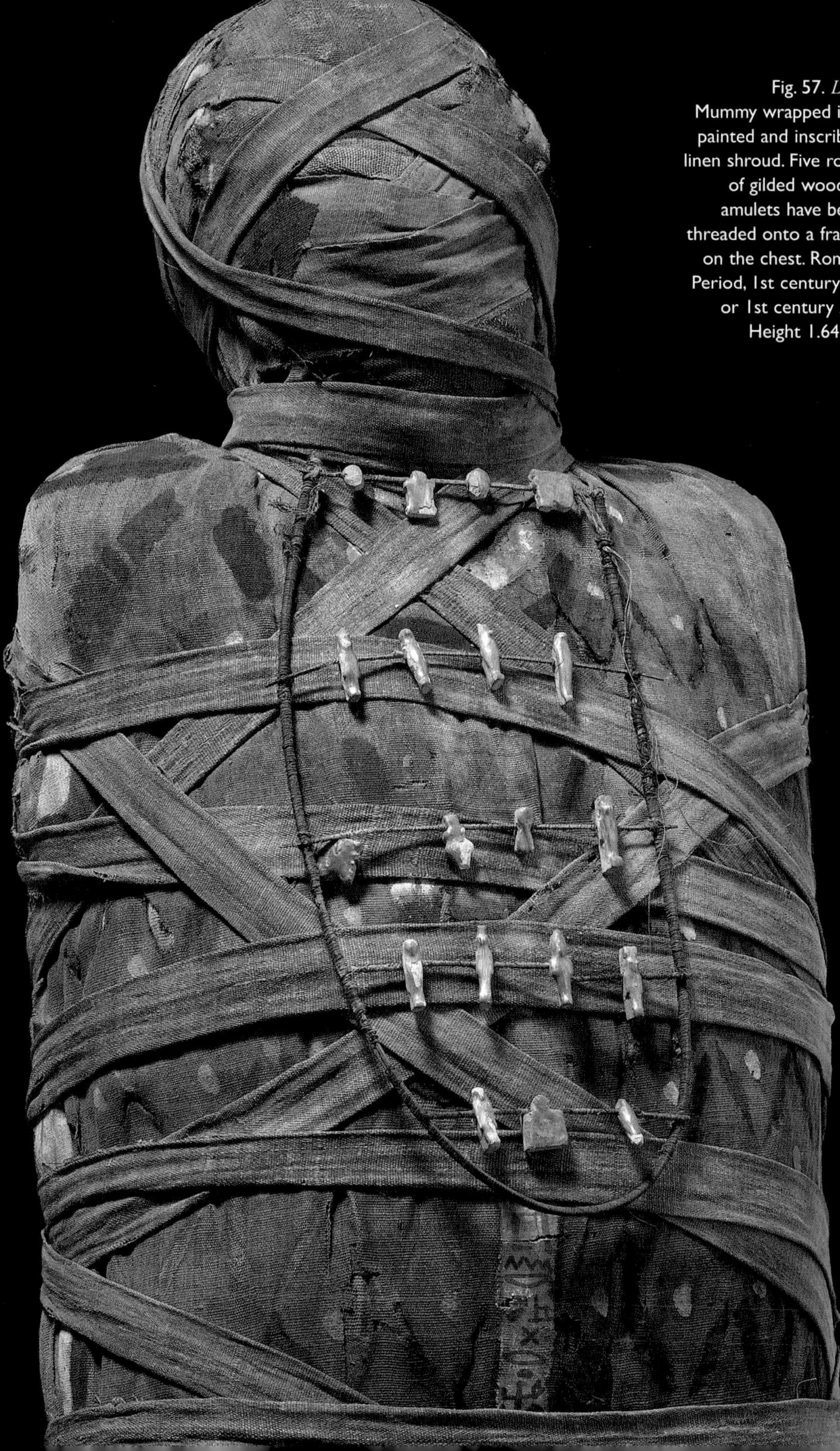

Fig. 57. *Left:*
Mummy wrapped in a
painted and inscribed
linen shroud. Five rows
of gilded wooden
amulets have been
threaded onto a frame
on the chest. Roman
Period, 1st century BC
or 1st century AD.
Height 1.64 m.

Fig. 58. *Right:* Hypocephalus of Neshorpakhered, covered with magical images of deities, including the sun god and the *ihet*-cow. Spell 162 of the *Book of the Dead* prescribed that these objects should be placed beneath the head of the mummy to create fire which would restore life to the dead. From Thebes, 4th–3rd century BC. Diameter 14 cm.

and in one of these battles Horus's left eye was plucked out. The god Thoth healed the eye and returned it to Horus, an act which is reflected in the name *wedjat,* meaning 'that which is whole'. As time passed, Horus the Elder came to be equated with a different Horus, the son of Osiris, and the *wedjat* eye became associated with him. As an amulet it was believed to possess strong powers to convey protection and well-being. *Wedjat* eyes made of many different materials were placed between the wrappings of mummies. A *wedjat* eye was often represented on a wax or metal plate which was placed over the incision made in the abdomen to extract the viscera during mummification; in this context the image probably acted as a means of 'healing' the wound and making the body whole again (see fig. 26, page 37).

Another common type of amulet was the scarab, a representation of the dung beetle *scarabaeus sacer.* The beetle was associated with the sun god and hence symbolized the renewal of life. In addition to the many small scarabs which were placed on mummies there was also usually a large scarab amulet which was ideally made of dark green stone (see fig. 94, page 120). On its base was often inscribed a spell from the *Book of the Dead* (usually spell 30B) which prevented the heart of the deceased testifying against its owner at the judgement (see page 120). These 'heart scarabs' were sometimes placed within the mummy's chest or under the wrappings on the breast.

Other frequent amulets included the snake's head, which provided cool refreshment at the throat, the two fingers of the embalmer god Anubis, to protect the abdominal incision, the papyrus column, a guarantee of eternal youth, and the headrest, which promoted resurrection after death and guarded against the loss of the head. In the Ptolemaic Period a disc of linen known as a hypocephalus was placed under the heads of some mummies. These items were also of amuletic significance and were covered with inscriptions and images of deities. They served to kindle life-giving fire under the head of the deceased.

The basic range of amulets was greatly expanded in the first millennium BC. Many small images in stone and faience were placed between the layers of bandages, particularly on the throat and chest, traditionally regarded as the most vulnerable areas of the body. Scarabs, *wedjat* eyes, *djed* pillars and figurines of deities were among the commonest. In the Late and Ptolemaic periods the amulets were laid out in carefully composed schemes, sometimes in two layers within the wrappings of a single mummy.

Fig. 59. *Below:* Faience figures of the four Sons of Horus. The holes at head and foot show that they were originally attached to a network of beads which would have been placed over the outer wrappings of the mummy. Provenance unknown. Late Period, 600–300 BC. Heights 4.0–4.6 cm.

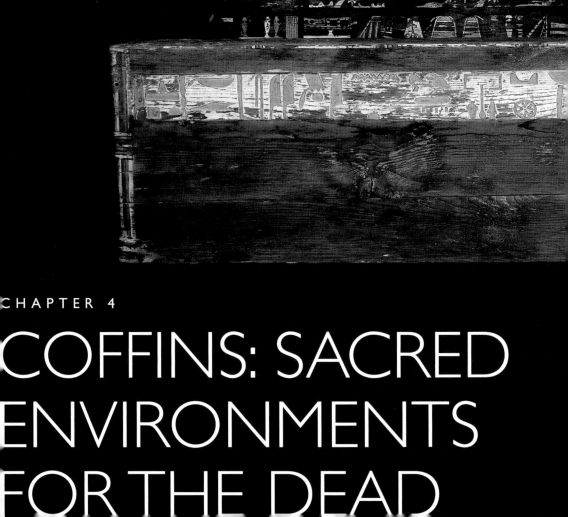

CHAPTER 4

COFFINS: SACRED ENVIRONMENTS FOR THE DEAD

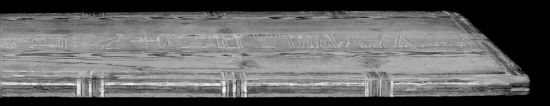

Fig. 60. *This page:*
Cedar wood inner
coffin of a middle-
ranking official named
Sebekhetepi. The eyes
painted on the eastern-
facing side were to
enable the occupant to
look towards the rising
sun. The inscription is
an offering formula
addressed to Osiris.
From tomb 723 at
Beni Hasan. Late 11th
Dynasty, c.2000 BC.
Length 1.86 m.

IN EGYPTIAN BURIALS OF THE EARLIEST PERIOD, and in those of the poor at all times, the body was laid to rest directly in the grave, without any container. But in the late fourth millennium BC coffins started to be provided, and over the next 3500 years a coffin became the most essential item of funerary furniture for those who could afford one. There was an astonishing variety and richness in their appearance.

While a humble peasant could expect no more than a roughly made box of unpainted wood or woven reeds, the mummy of a king such as Tutankhamun was placed in a series of human-shaped coffins of intricate workmanship, one inside the other, the innermost being of solid gold. The great diversity of coffin decoration reflected evolving religious attitudes, for an Egyptian coffin was much more than a simple container: it was endowed with powerful symbolic meaning, which helped its occupant to be resurrected and to flourish in the life after death. Like the tomb in which it lay, the coffin provided a sacred environment for the eternal life of its occupant – it was a dwelling, a shrine, the body of the mother-goddess Nut (see page 80), and even a miniature replica of the entire cosmos. All of these roles were alluded to by the coffin's shape, its colour and the inscriptions and images on its surfaces.

Early Egyptian coffins were often baskets made from bundles of reeds, or simple boxes constructed from wooden planks. Others were made of clay – either large storage jars recycled as containers for the body, or simple ceramic boxes. The wooden chests were only about one metre long and were constructed in this form to hold the body in a contracted posture. Some of them had slightly vaulted lids and a repeated pattern of recessed panelling on the sides. These features were based on the architecture of the great tombs and funerary 'palaces' of the time, structures which were meant to act as houses for the deceased and as places in which human existence would be eternally renewed. Reproducing this symbolic decoration on the coffin enabled it to serve as a miniature version of one of these great tombs.

Developments in mummification procedures led to changes in the style of coffins. By the early years of the Old Kingdom the bodies of elite persons were prepared for burial in the fully extended position, and to accommodate these longer mummies coffins were increased in length. Both wooden coffins and stone sarcophagi began to be produced with these proportions, sometimes having architectural decoration of the type described above.

Towards the end of the Old Kingdom a new type of coffin was introduced. It had a flat lid, smooth sides and distinctive decoration which reflected its religious significance. When the coffin was placed in the tomb it was to be positioned with the head pointing north and the feet south. The mummy was not usually laid on

Fig. 61. *Opposite:* One of the earliest Egyptian coffins, a simple rectangular wooden box with a flat lid. These coffins were usually around one metre in length and contained a body in a contracted posture. In this case the skeleton is that of a young adult female. From tomb 1955 at Tarkhan. 1st Dynasty, c.3000 BC. Length 91.2 cm.

Fig. 62. *Right:* Red granite sarcophagus with a vaulted lid and a repeated panelling design on the sides. On the eastern face a false door was carved at each end to allow the spirit to move freely in and out. From Giza. Probably 5th Dynasty, c.2494–2395 BC. Length 2.25 m.

its back but on its left side, and the head was supported in a raised position by means of a headrest which was placed on the floor of the coffin. Through this arrangement the corpse was symbolically likened to a sleeping person who would awaken to new life. It also meant that the deceased faced in an easterly direction, looking towards the horizon where the sun, the symbol of resurrection, would rise each dawn. The burial chamber might be located deep underground and surrounded by solid rock, but this was not regarded as an obstacle to the contact between the solar rays and the mummy. However, to make doubly sure that the

dead person was able to see, a pair of eyes was usually painted, carved or inlaid on the eastern side of the coffin at the end where the head was located. These eyes could serve the deceased by magic as efficiently as real eyes, and within the coffin the mummy's face was carefully positioned so as to be aligned with them.

Because the coffin was a sacred environment or dwelling for the deceased it was thought that he or she could leave it and re-enter it in spirit form. Other images on the surfaces were designed to make this easier. On many rectangular coffins of the Middle Kingdom a doorway was painted on the east side, just below the 'eye panel'. Sometimes another door was represented on the inner surface, but both are depicted closed and bolted. A similar type of 'false door' was often carved in stone and placed in the tomb chapel where the spirit was to receive its offerings. Whether on the coffin or in the chapel, the purpose of the door was the same – to act as a magical portal through which the disembodied spirit could pass. It was an interface between the world of the living and that of the dead.

During the Old and Middle Kingdoms hieroglyphic inscriptions were usually written or carved on the sides and lid of the coffin. Many of these were addresses to gods such as Osiris and Anubis, requesting them to provide an endless supply of food and drink and other necessities to keep the deceased from hunger, thirst or want of any kind. Other inscriptions were concise references to rituals which were performed at the time of the burial. Some of these rituals involved re-enacting mythical events, with priests carrying out the roles of gods and goddesses. These deities are often named in columns of text located at intervals along the sides of the coffin. Isis and Nephthys, the sisters of Osiris, are regularly included, as are Geb, Nut, Shu and Tefnut, the personifications of earth, sky, air and moisture in one of the main Egyptian stories of creation, and the Sons of Horus. In the rituals, these deities were supposed to attend on Ra or Osiris, and the deceased inside the coffin was identified with one or both of those supreme gods. Through this identification the deceased himself became a powerful creator-god who wielded the ability to renew life.

Such was the Egyptians' belief in the creative power of the written word that by inscribing these texts on the coffin the rites they evoked would be perpetuated for all eternity, ensuring the survival of the deceased. Images were considered to be no less powerful than words. The most important texts and images were located inside the coffin, in closest proximity to the mummy, so that the dead person would have direct access to them. Some of the most striking examples are in coffins of the Middle Kingdom, which contain a wealth of internal decoration. A false door and an offering table loaded with food and drink are often painted there, allowing the spirit free passage in and out and also a plentiful supply of sustenance. There are also often narrow pictorial strips along the upper edges of the coffin walls, 'object friezes' which contain small but detailed images of granaries, clothes and sandals, items of jewellery, furniture, vessels, tools and weapons and other goods which were thought appropriate to the afterlife of a person of high rank. All these pictures, by magic, could become reality. Interestingly, the object friezes also reflect the occupants' aspirations to attain higher status in the afterlife. They often include headdresses and sceptres which would have been available only to the king in life; after death they were

Fig. 63. *Opposite:* Outer coffin of the physician, Gua (see page 53). It is made of imported cedar wood and the interior is covered with funerary images and inscriptions from the *Coffin Texts*, including the separate composition known as the *Book of Two Ways*. From Deir el-Bersha. 12th Dynasty, c.1870 BC. Length 261.7 cm.

appropriate for non-royal persons as well, helping to equate them with Osiris, ruler of the netherworld.

The occupant of the coffin also needed special knowledge, which would equip him for his journey to the realm of the dead and enable him to avoid disaster along the way. To meet this need, large sections of the coffin's surfaces were inscribed with spells in vertical columns, written in ink. These are known to Egyptologists as the *Coffin Texts*.

The *Coffin Texts* belonged to a tradition of funerary literature which was originally reserved for the king. The earliest selection, the *Pyramid Texts,* were inscribed on the walls of the burial chambers of royal pyramids in the late Old Kingdom. In the First Intermediate Period, this corpus of spells, greatly expanded as the *Coffin Texts,* and became available for the king's subjects to use as well. The spells provided the deceased with information about the realm he was to enter.

Some of the spells took the form of 'guides to the hereafter.' Among these was a self-contained group of spells which had the ancient name the *Book of Two Ways.* It was accompanied by a complex diagram, rather like a map, in which paths and watercourses are marked out and labelled with their names to enable the deceased to find his way safely to the blessed realm. The diagram was drawn on the base-board of the coffin, as though it were the actual ground under the feet of the occupant – a reflection of the concept that the coffin's surfaces defined a miniature universe around the dead person.

Until the late 11th Dynasty (about 2000 BC), all Egyptian coffins were rectangular chests. But at that time a new type of case, the anthropoid or mummy-shaped coffin, was introduced. In later centuries it was to become the dominant type. The early anthropoid coffins were made of wood or cartonnage, and were quite simple in design. In appearance they reproduced the iconography of the mummy very closely, with face mask and collar represented and sometimes a short inscription in the centre. The background was often a uniform white (like linen wrappings) or black (a colour which symbolized resurrection), though some specimens have elaborate patterning representing a network of beads. There was no internal decoration because these cases acted as the outer shell of the mummified body; as in earlier periods mummies were placed on their left sides within rectangular coffins.

In the Second Intermediate Period Egypt underwent a temporary political division into several kingdoms. One consequence of this was the development of different regional styles of coffin. In the area of Thebes a new type of anthropoid coffin was introduced. They are distinguished by their unusually large headdresses and by the use of a pattern of feathers to decorate the lid. From this they derive their modern name, *Rishi* coffins (from an Arabic word for 'feather').

Fig. 64.

Opposite and above: Anthropoid *Rishi* coffin of King Nubkheperre Intef, carved from the wood of the sycamore fig. The exterior of the lid was gilded and the interior coated with a dark resinous substance. The central inscription is a prayer requesting a good burial. From Dra Abu el-Naga, Thebes. 17th Dynasty, c.1600 BC. Height 1.92 m.

A large pair of wings appears to be stretched along the front of these coffins, ending above the feet. On some examples the wings begin near the top of the head, where there is a pattern of smaller feathers resembling the plumage of a falcon's body. At around the same time, similar decoration appeared on mummy masks, some of which have very small bird-like faces, and this has led to a suggestion that the *Rishi* coffins and masks depict the deceased in the form of the human-faced *ba*. According to an alternative hypothesis, the wings may represent the protection of the goddesses Isis and Nephthys.

Many *Rishi* coffins were hollowed from trunks of trees native to Egypt, such as the sycamore fig. Those made for private individuals are often crudely carved with grotesque, wedge-shaped faces. However, the coffins of several kings and queens of this period have been found in the Theban necropolis, and these are of much finer workmanship. One in the British Museum belonged to king Nubkheperre Intef, who reigned about 1600 BC (see pages 82–3). Though clumsy in its proportions it has a finely carved face with inlaid eyes, and the feathered decoration has been skilfully carved into a plastered surface overlaid

with gold leaf. The interior was thickly coated with a sticky black resin which had not yet dried when the mummy was put inside. Today one can still see part of the king's linen shroud stuck to the resin, and also a number of carrion beetles which had perhaps been feeding on the poorly embalmed body.

With the return of strong, centralized government in the New Kingdom, the coffins of kings continued to use the *Rishi* design in a modified form. The motif of large wings was replaced by a repeating pattern of feathers which shrouded the body like a garment, over which figures of deities were represented in attitudes of protection. Tutankhamun's tomb revealed the surprising complexity and richness of a royal burial ensemble at the height of the New Kingdom. The mummy lay within three coffins – the innermost of solid gold and the others of gilded and inlaid wood. These were placed inside a quartzite sarcophagus, surrounded by four gilded shrines. Each of these containers could act as a separate 'cosmos', and the use of multiple layers around the body emphasized its sacred nature.

Fig. 65. *Above:* Anthropoid grey granite coffin of Merymose. All three of Merymose's coffins were made of hard stone, a reflection of his high status. The texts and images are drawn from spells 151 and 161 of the *Book of the Dead*, and represent various gods, including Anubis and Thoth, protecting the deceased. From Thebes. 18th Dynasty, reign of Amenhotep III, c.1370 BC. Length 1.98 m.

Coffins for private individuals followed a rather different evolutionary path to those of the pharaohs. The anthropoid type predominated, and the coffins were usually made from planks of wood held together by wooden tongues and dowels. The exterior decorated surfaces were divided into compartments by lines of inscription, an arrangement adopted from the earlier rectangular coffins. The spaces between these bands were at first left blank, but later were filled with funerary scenes or figures of deities.

These images represented the gods who were named in the inscriptions; besides eternalizing the important funerary rituals, they provided a kind of cordon of divine protection around the mummy. The background colour of the coffins changed through time – first white, then black, and later yellow. Each colour scheme possessed different religious meaning: white for the shroud-like garment in which the dead were regenerated, black (the colour of the fertile silt of the Nile floodplain) as a symbol of new life, and yellow to suggest the golden glow imparted by the rejuvenating rays of the sun. But for persons of very high status the surface of the coffin might be partly or wholly covered with gold leaf, as in the case of Henutmehyt.

This lady, probably a member of a wealthy family, was buried in two anthropoid coffins, one fitting inside the other. Over her linen wrappings lay a 'mummy board', resembling a mask which was extended to cover the body from head to foot, the lower part adorned with figures of gods like those on the coffins. These boards replaced the mummy-mask in the later years of the New Kingdom and became a standard element of burial equipment in the 21st Dynasty.

In the Third Intermediate Period economic pressures brought about a decline in the richness of burials. The tombs of several kings of the 21st and 22nd Dynasties have been discovered at Tanis in the Delta, but compared with the wealth found in Tutankhamun's sepulchre the burial equipment of these later rulers seems rather meagre. They were forced to recycle stone sarcophagi of earlier periods, but the coffins placed inside them were newly made. Some of these were of gilded wood, while others were of silver. They were anthropoid in shape, but on some the human face of the king was replaced by the head of a falcon, probably representing the funerary god Sokar-Osiris.

On account of the shortage of resources at this time there was an increased tendency to concentrate many burials in one spot and to reuse older tombs. Few people were able to have tombs decorated for their sole use, and in consequence the coffin assumed a more important role in creating the sacred space in which the occupant would be eternally reborn. The coffins made for private individuals in the 21st Dynasty were of wood, and have a distinctive colour scheme of red, green and blue on a yellow background. The predominant yellow colour was

Fig. 66. *Left:* Inner coffin of Henutmehyt made of gilded tamarisk wood, with a painted wig and inlaid eyes. The crossed arms identify the dead woman with Osiris. She wears a pectoral ornament and a collar, and on the breast is a winged figure of the goddess Nut. From Thebes. 19th Dynasty, c.1250 BC. Height 1.93 m, width 50 cm.

Fig. 67. *Right:*
Coffin of the priest of
Amun Bakenmut. The
bright yellow varnish
and the many small
figures of gods and
divine emblems are
typical of the 21st
Dynasty. The hands,
emerging through a
deep floral collar, grasp
the *djed* and *tit* (Isis-
knot) emblems. From
Deir el-Bahri, cache of
the priests of Amun.
21st Dynasty, *c.*970 BC.
Length 2.08 m.

Fig. **68**. *Opposite:*
Cartonnage case
containing the mummy
of a woman named
Tjentmutengebtiu. The
face is gilded, and the
scenes on the front
show the deceased
before Osiris, the
Abydos fetish and *djed*
pillar (symbols of
Osiris), and the
deceased receiving
libations of life-giving
water from Horus and
Thoth. From Thebes.
Early 22nd Dynasty,
*c.*900 BC. Height 1.69 m.

Fig. 69. *Above:*
Cartonnage case
containing the mummy of
a girl named Tjayasetimu.
It is unusual in depicting
the arms and feet freed
from the wrappings. The
inscriptions and figures
of deities were obscured
by a dark, resinous
coating. 22nd Dynasty,
c.800 BC. Height 1.51 m.

Fig. 70. *Right:* Cartonnage case containing the mummy of a man named Djedameniufankh. The rear opening was secured by means of string threaded through holes. The lozenge-shaped pattern imitates a network of beads. 22nd Dynasty, c.800 BC. Height 1.81 m.

enhanced by liberal coatings of varnish on the surfaces. It continued the tradition of the late New Kingdom, symbolizing the glowing brightness of the sun's rays, which were supposed to renew the life of the dead person when they shone upon them. The surfaces of these coffins are divided into small compartments and are densely covered with images of gods, scarab beetles and other symbols of rebirth. By this time, the interior of the anthropoid coffin case was also regularly occupied by images. In these there was a strong emphasis on the roles played by Osiris and Ra in bringing new life, and on the interrelationship between the two gods, who were viewed as two aspects of one supreme creator.

New styles of coffin were introduced in the 22nd Dynasty. The mummy was now regularly enclosed within a snugly fitting case made of cartonnage (see page 156). The mummy was inserted into the case through a rear opening which was afterwards closed by a lacing of string threaded through holes, like a shoe or corset. The outer surface of the case, finely plastered, was covered with religious images in bright colours. These were sometimes arranged in rectangular compartments and showed divine emblems and often a scene in which the deceased is welcomed by the gods after passing through judgement (see chapter 5). Other cartonnage cases were painted with variations on a scene representing the rebirth of the sun. A figure of the sun god at dawn – usually a ram-headed falcon – was depicted above the fetish of Abydos, which represented Osiris. The scene represented the moment when the sun rose, reborn into the sky from the subterranean netherworld (the kingdom of Osiris) where it

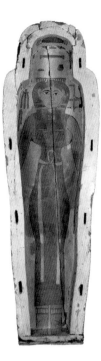

Fig. 71. *Left and above:* Coffin of Nesmut, inside which is painted an unusual full-face figure of Nut, goddess of the sky and mother of Osiris. She was symbolically equated with the coffin, in which the dead person lay like a child in the womb, ready for rebirth. From Thebes. 25th Dynasty, c.700–675 BC. Height 1.85 m.

Fig. 72. *Right:* Mummiform siltstone coffin of the vizier Sasobek. He holds the *tit* and *djed* emblems, and a figure of the goddess Nut is carved on the breast. Early 26th Dynasty, c.630 BC. Height 2.23 m.

had passed the night. The embracing wings of the solar falcon also recalled the *ba* uniting with the mummy (see page 11), an event crucial to the renewal of life.

The cartonnage cases were placed inside wooden coffins, anthropoid in shape but of a rather simple design. Decoration was sparse, but a common motif is the figure of Nut, the eternal mother and personification of the sky, which is often drawn on the inside of the coffin. Her arms are outstretched so that she appears to embrace the mummy. The coffin, in fact, was often equated with the body of Nut so that when the deceased was placed inside it, he or she was symbolically

Fig. 73. *Left and above:* Inner coffin of the priest of Montu, Besenmut. The entire surface, inside and out, is covered with inscriptions, most of which are extracts from the *Book of the Dead.* Surrounding the mummy with these magical texts not only provided protection but gave Besenmut direct access to the spells in order to use them himself. From Thebes, 25th–26th Dynasties, c.650 BC. Height 1.88 m.

93

Fig. 74. *Right:* Outer and inner coffins of Hor, priest of Montu. The rectangular outer coffin represents the cosmos, with a vaulted lid imitating the sky arched above the earth. Figures of protective deities are painted along the sides. From Thebes. 25th Dynasty, c.700–675 BC. Length 2.15 m.

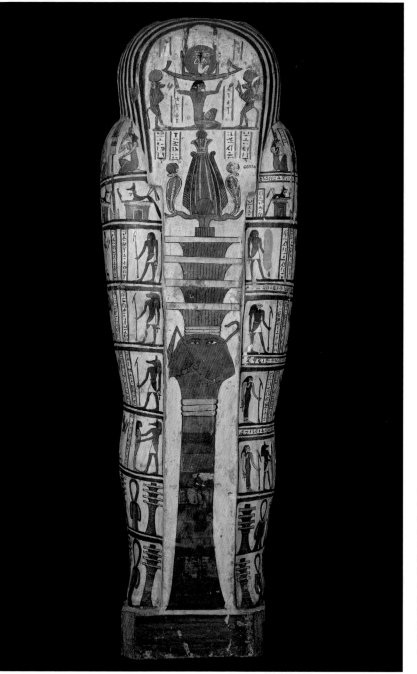

Fig. 75. *Opposite:*
Coffin of Pasenhor, a
member of the Libyan
Meshwesh tribe. The
lid recreates the
weighing of the heart
scene before Osiris,
with the dead man
being presented to
the gods. Included are
text extracts from the
'negative confession', in
which he demonstrates
his good character by
denying that he is guilty
of 42 specific sins.
From Thebes. Early
25th Dynasty, c.725 BC.
Height 2.03 m.

Fig. 76. *Left:*
Rear of the coffin of
Itineb. The central
image is the *djed* pillar
with a human torso
and eyes and the
crown and sceptres
of Osiris. Above, the
sun disc in a barque
is raised into the sky
at dawn. Both sides
are covered with
figures of deities and
protective emblems.
Saqqara. Late Period,
c.600–300 BC. Height
1.83 m.

within the womb of the mother goddess, and prepared for rebirth. The exterior decoration of these coffins sometimes shows a different theme – that of a series of protective deities who surround the mummy to ward off evil forces. Some wooden coffins of this period have decoration which focuses on the judgement (see page 120).

The weighing of the heart and the presentation of the deceased to Osiris or Ra are painted on the breast, and below is the text of the denial of sins through which the good character of the dead person was demonstrated to the gods. Perhaps these coffins were supposed to symbolically recreate the hall of judgement, as one of the microcosms in which the deceased would find himself, thereby ensuring that the crucial moment of vindication was eternally re-enacted.

A new type of anthropoid coffin was introduced in the 25th Dynasty to serve as the mummy's inner casing. These coffins represent the mummy standing on a rectangular plinth or pedestal, with a pillar supporting the back, so that the coffin resembles a statue. The external surfaces of many of these coffins were densely covered with inscriptions – often spells from the *Book of the Dead* – which dominate much of the space. Small-scale figures of gods are also included, and these continue the old tradition of reflecting important rituals, in this case the rite of defending the body of Osiris from the attacks of his enemy Seth during the night before the burial (see page 106).

These cases were usually enclosed within one or two outer coffins of wood. These were sometimes of anthropoid type, but for the wealthier owners a rectangular outer coffin was provided. With its vaulted lid and posts at the four corners, this type of coffin reproduced the appearance of a shrine, the appropriate earthly dwelling for a divine being. However, this was not the only symbolic role of such a coffin, for it also served as a model of the cosmos. The curved top was equated with the sky, and appropriately often bore images of the solar barque being towed along by deities. The four posts were interpreted as the supports which the Egyptians believed held the sky in place; these 'corners' of the heavens were often represented by four falcons either painted on the coffin lid or carved as wooden statuettes, to be placed, one on top of each post, in the burial chamber.

During the 25th and 26th Dynasties, these coffin styles were very popular in Upper Egypt, particularly at Thebes. Similar coffins were used at sites in the northern part of Egypt, but here stone sarcophagi were more widespread. These sarcophagi of anthropoid type continued in use up to the Ptolemaic Period alongside the more traditional wooden coffins. Many of these later examples have distinctive proportions with an over-large head and a swollen torso. The decorative repertoire became rather restricted, with fewer long inscriptions and a tendency to repeat a small selection of standard images: the mummy lying on a

Fig. **78**. *Above:* Breccia sarcophagus made for Nectanebo II. The surfaces are covered with texts and images from the *Book of Amduat.* The sarcophagus was never used for the king's burial and was later installed in a mosque in Alexandria as a receptacle for water. The holes were drilled at that time to enable the sarcophagus to be emptied periodically. 30th Dynasty, *c.*350 BC. Length 3.13 m.

bier, the Sons of Horus and the winged figure of the goddess Nut are among the most common.

The cultural diversity of Egyptian society in the Roman Period (30 BC–AD 395) was manifested in the trappings of mummies as well as the design of coffins. The traditions of pharaonic Egypt and the Graeco-Roman world now coexisted side by side. Some burials had idealized cartonnage mummy-masks and coffins of anthropoid or rectangular shape decorated with a predominantly Egyptian repertoire of images, such as figures of deities, winged solar discs and scarab beetles. At the same time, other mummies were adorned with realistic plaster masks or wooden portrait panels depicting the deceased wearing the costume, hairstyles and jewellery fashionable in the Roman world. Complete coffins of wood and cartonnage also represented the deceased in this style, and yet hybrid images of the dead were also available. Both coffins and shrouds combine a Classical image of the deceased with figures of Egyptian gods.

Fig. 79. *Left and above:* Gilded and painted mummy-case made of recycled papyrus covered with plaster and linen. The lid represents the dead woman in an elaborate costume, with a floral garland and sandals. Features such as the meander pattern on the sleeves are of Greek origin. Akhmim. Late 1st century BC or early 1st century AD. Height 1.65 m.

Fig. 80. *Right:* Interior of the lid of the painted wooden coffin of Soter, an official of Thebes. Pharaonic Egyptian tradition is seen in the vaulted shape of the coffin and the full-face image of the goddess Nut, but Roman influence is responsible for the inclusion of the signs of the zodiac on each side of the goddess. Thebes. Early 2nd century AD. Height 2.13 m.

Fig. 81. *Left:*
Painted mummy-cover of Pakhons. A plaster mask is attached to a linen base. The dead man wears a Roman-style tunic and holds a cup and a garland of flowers. The wooden label attached to the mummy (see page 52) identified the deceased and named his home-village as Terkythis, probably located on the Theban west bank. 3rd century AD. Height 86 cm, width 33.5 cm.

CHAPTER 5

RITUALS, TOMBS AND THE DESTINY OF THE DEAD

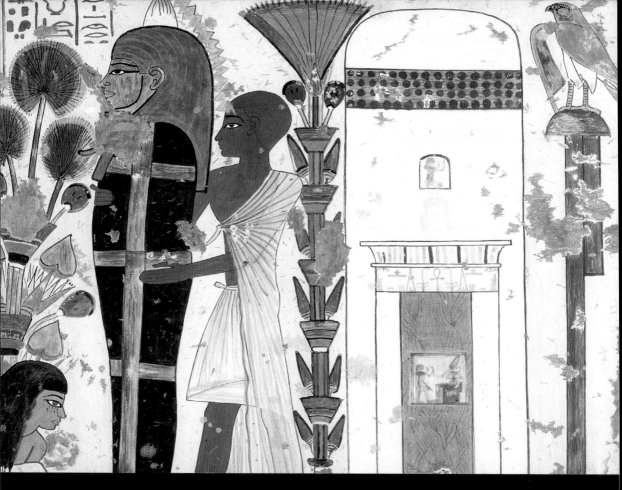

Fig. 82. *Above:*
Funerary rituals performed
on two mummies outside
the tomb on the day of
burial. Painting from the
tomb of Nebamun and
Ipuky at Thebes. Late 18th
Dynasty, c.1380 BC.
Facsimile by Nina Davies.

THE PERIOD WHICH ELAPSED between death and burial in ancient Egypt was traditionally seventy days. At the end of this time the corpse, mummified and provided with all its trappings, was taken to the tomb.

Since the artificial preservation of the body could be completed in a shorter period it seems that the seventy days was chosen because it symbolized the renewal of life; the decans – groups of stars which the Egyptians associated with gods – disappeared below the horizon for a period of seventy days before emerging again apparently regenerated.

The mummification process had been governed by ritual, and the sequence of rituals culminated in the day of burial, when the mummy would be reanimated. Great care was taken to protect the body on the night before the funeral. A vigil was maintained around it as it lay on its bier to guard it from the hostile intentions of the god Seth and his agents. On the day of burial the mummy was conveyed to the tomb in a long procession. Many wall-scenes in tombs and vignettes on papyri depict this procession. The mummy is shown under a shrine-like canopy, drawn on a sledge pulled by oxen.

Fig. 83. *Below:* The procession to the tomb. The mummy, on a model boat, is drawn on a sledge by oxen and attendants. A priest burns incense and the widow laments. At the rear, servants bring the canopic chest and objects to be placed in the tomb. *Book of the Dead,* papyrus of Ani. Thebes. 19th Dynasty, c.1275 BC. Height 42 cm.

Behind it follow the viscera in a canopic chest and the possessions of the deceased – chairs, stools, beds, clothing, jewellery and even chariots – carried by servants. There is often a mysterious bundle called the *tekenu,* sometimes shown with a human head, the purpose of which is uncertain. It may have contained the portions of the corpse which were not included in the wrapped mummy and the canopic jars but which nevertheless required proper disposal. A prominent role in the funeral was also played by a group of female mourners who, with dishevelled hair and exposed breasts, gesticulated and beat themselves with their hands, giving vent to loud cries of lamentation.

When the cortege reached the tomb the mummy was placed upright on a small heap of clean sand. Further rituals were performed, the chief part being traditionally taken by the eldest son, who in this way confirmed his status as the legitimate heir to the property of the deceased. The most important ritual was the 'Opening of the Mouth'. Its purpose was to reanimate the mummy so that the spirit could re-enter it and the individual could once more breathe, see, hear, speak and receive nourishment. In order to implement this, the mouth of

the mummy-mask (or the face of the anthropoid inner coffin) was touched with a variety of ritual objects which symbolically 'opened' the apertures of the head. This ritual can be traced back to Egypt's prehistory. One of the tools used was a knife called the *pesesh-kef* which had a bifurcated blade resembling a fish-tail. Examples of these knives have been found in graves of the Nagada I period (*c.*4000–3500 BC). Originally the ritual may have been based on practices which were carried out at birth, such as clearing the baby's mouth of mucus to enable it to breathe and cutting the umbilical cord. It was probably thought that to perform these acts symbolically on the dead would restore them to life. As time passed, new elements were added to the ritual. During the New Kingdom many of the implements used were craftsmen's tools such as adzes and chisels, and these probably owed their inclusion to the custom of performing an 'opening of the mouth' on statues in order to enable them to receive the spirit of the person represented. The merging of the animation-rites for mummies and statues is not surprising: they shared a common function as vessels for the spiritual components of the owner.

But whereas the statue was to be animated for the first time, the mummy was to be reanimated. The ritual also involved the presentation of food-offerings to the deceased. Among these a highly important one was the foreleg of a calf, freshly cut from the animal and offered to the mummy while the life-force still pulsated within it. It was not merely food for the dead, but the giving of life itself.

Fig. 84. *Opposite:* Anubis supports the mummy while female relatives mourn for the deceased, and priests perform the Opening of the Mouth. *Book of the Dead,* papyrus of Hunefer. Thebes, 19th Dynasty, *c.*1280 BC. Height 39 cm.

Fig. 85. *Below:* Set of model implements for performing the Opening of the Mouth ritual: models of cups and jars, a bifurcated *pesesh-kef* knife and two blades (one is missing) called *netjerwy.* From Abydos, 6th Dynasty, *c.*2300 BC. Height 17.7 cm.

Fig. 86. *Left:* Painted wooden model of butchers preparing meat for the owner of the tomb. Two cows have been slaughtered and the butchers are cutting the meat into joints. Such models would magically guarantee an eternal supply of food for the dead. From Deir el-Bersha. 12th Dynasty, *c.*1870 BC. Length 43.5 cm.

Fig. **87**. *Right:*
An official's tomb of
the Old Kingdom,
c.2650 BC, with a
stone superstructure
containing a chapel for
funerary rituals, and a
vertical shaft leading
to a subterranean
burial chamber.

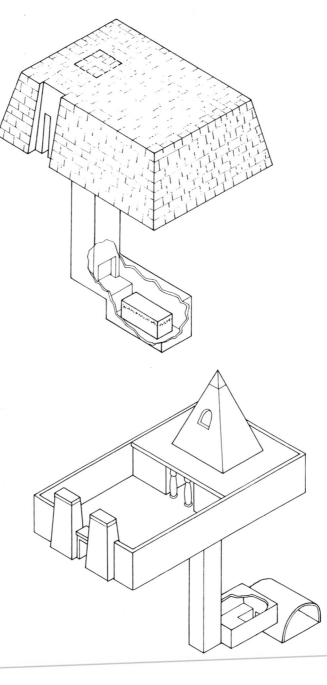

Fig. **88**. *Right:*
Tomb of a high-
ranking person of the
later New Kingdom,
c.1300–1100 BC. A
pylon gateway leads
to a courtyard, open
to the sun, and a
chapel with a small
pyramid above. A shaft
leads to the burial
apartments below.

Once the rituals were completed, the mummy was carried to the subterranean burial chamber and placed in its coffins. If a stone sarcophagus had been provided this would have been installed in the tomb in advance. The grave goods were also put in place. In the pharaohs' tombs of the New Kingdom separate rooms were allotted for different categories of funerary equipment, but for persons of lower rank the items were usually laid on the floor of the burial chamber or on top of the coffin. These final acts in the funeral were supposed to be performed with reverence, but sometimes those responsible for sealing the tomb took advantage of their position to steal valuables. In a few burials which have been found undisturbed, gold masks had been ripped from coffins and the mummy itself rifled for the sake of its jewellery before the tomb was closed.

The tomb, as the physical setting for the afterlife, was of supreme importance to the Egyptians. Their writings frequently emphasize the desirability of preparing a lasting burial place: 'The house of death is for life'. It is often described as the 'house of eternity'. It was not simply the resting place of the corpse but the interface between the world of the living and that of the resurrected dead. Whereas the dwellings of the living were transitory and were built of perishable mud, timber and reed, the tomb was to last for eternity and was therefore built, if possible, of stone. The size and character of tombs varied over time and in accordance with the status of their owners. The pyramids of the kings Khufu, Khafre and Menkaure at Giza were the greatest and most labour-intensive structures ever built to house a single corpse, while their humblest subjects would have been buried in simple pit-graves, dug into the ground at the desert edge. But all Egyptian tombs comprised two parts, each of which fulfilled a key function: a burial chamber in which the dead

Fig. 89. *Below:* Clay model of a dwelling with offerings of food placed in the courtyard. Such 'soul houses' were included in the burials of people who were unable to afford a stone-built tomb chapel. They provided a home and symbolic nourishment for the spirit. 12th Dynasty, c.1900 BC. Length 40.6 cm

body lay protected, and a cult-place where the spirit was nourished by offerings.

In a simple burial the offerings might be placed on the surface above the grave-pit, but for a person of high status the cult would be performed in a chapel – either in a free-standing stone superstructure or in a series of chambers cut into the rock. In both these types of tomb the burial chamber was located below the chapel, with which it communicated by means of a vertical shaft.

In order to sustain the *ka* of the tomb owner, food and drink were brought to the chapel and placed on an offering table, while incense was burned and the words of the liturgy were recited. The focus of the cult was a statue of the owner, which was placed either openly in the chapel or concealed in a nearby walled-up chamber called a serdab. The *ka* of the owner entered the statue and was then able to receive nourishment from the offerings. The feeding of the *ka* was important if the individual were to survive beyond death, and this was the main purpose of the mortuary cult. Ideally, offerings were to be brought to the tomb for all eternity by the deceased's descendants, but in case the family became extinct or neglected their ancestors, the duty could be carried out by the priests of a temple, since the rituals of serving the gods and nourishing the dead were closely related. Hapidjefai of Asyut, a nobleman of the Middle Kingdom, entered into contracts with his local priests in an attempt to ensure that his mortuary cult would be maintained by them and their successors for as long as the temple existed. The conditions of these contracts were inscribed on the walls of the tomb chapel as a permanent record.

However, the Egyptians were realists enough to understand that in practice such cults would sooner or later fall into disuse. The deceased would then be thrown upon his own resources to avoid starvation. The solution was to equip the dead

Fig. 90. *Opposite:* Painted limestone figurine representing a naked woman and a child lying on a bed. Such images were sometimes placed in houses, to promote fertility and hence the continuation of the family. When placed in the tomb they aided the regeneration of the dead. 19th–20th Dynasties, c.1295–1069 BC. Length 23.5 cm.

Fig. 91. *Left:* Painted wooden figure of the god Osiris. These images were often hollow and served as containers for funerary papyri. This one held the *Book of the Dead*, papyrus of Hunefer (see page 108). Thebes, 19th Dynasty, c.1280 BC. Height 82 cm.

with magical texts and images which would ensure that basic necessities were perpetually available to them. For this reason the walls of tomb chapels and the surfaces of coffins and stelae were carved and painted with images of foodstuffs, clothing and other goods, and depictions of servants engaged in agricultural activities. From the late Old Kingdom to the Middle Kingdom, wooden models of servants fulfilled a similar function. Since both word and image were believed to have the capacity to become reality, the occupant of the tomb would never be without food and other comforts. Probably the commonest text written in tombs was the *hetep di nesu,* an offering formula, which requested supplies of bread, beer, oxen, fowl, linen, incense, wine, beer, milk and other commodities, usually in multiples of one thousand. The opening words, *hetep di nesu,* 'An offering which the king gives', refer to the belief that the king made offerings to satisfy the gods who, in turn, would supply the dead with everything they needed. The presence of these words inscribed in the tomb or on the coffin would alone be sufficient to bring the offerings into existence, but the preferred option was that the text should be spoken aloud. For this reason many tombs and stelae include an address to visitors or passers-by, entreating them to pronounce the formula for the benefit of the occupant.

Although the mummy and the *ka* were expected to remain in the tomb forever, the dead were thought to be able to move beyond the burial place to

Fig. 92. *Below:* Painted wooden model of a funerary boat. Beneath a canopy, the mummy lies on a bier, attended by a priest and by the goddesses Isis and Nephthys. The green colouring of the hull represents bundles of papyrus, of which such craft were made. The steering-oars and their poles are topped by falcon heads representing divinities. Thebes, 12th Dynasty, c.1850 BC. Length 77.5 cm.

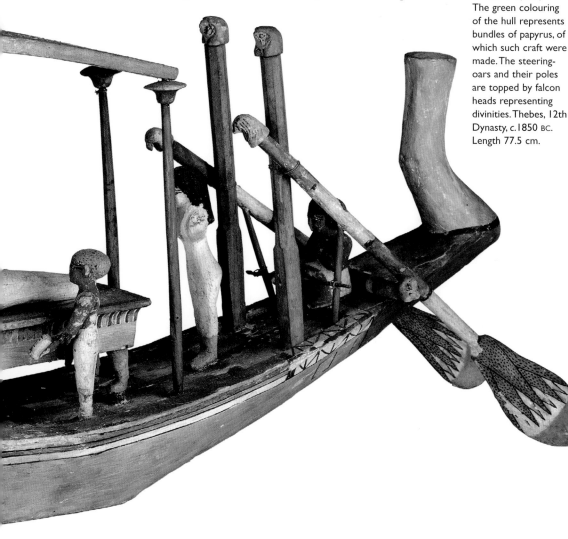

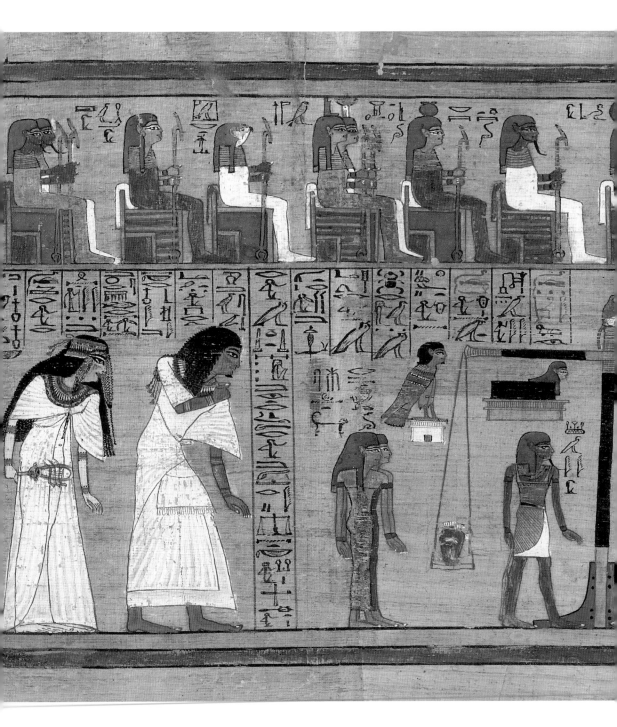

THE WEIGHING OF THE HEART

In the hall of judgement, the dead man had to call upon forty-two assessors who were seated around the hall, assuring each in turn that during his life he had been innocent of a specific misdeed. His heart was placed on the scale-pan of a balance and weighed against an image of *Maat*, the concept of right and order. The heart was regarded as the centre of the person's being, his mind, and it held a record of his deeds on earth. The weighing also determined whether or not he had lived according to the principles of truth and correct behaviour. If the heart and the *Maat* image balanced correctly he was vindicated and declared *maa-kheru*, literally 'true of voice'. If the balance was unsatisfactory the heart was swallowed by the Devourer, a hybrid monster, part crocodile, part lion, part hippopotamus. This 'second death' resulted in the total and final extinction of the individual. To add to the tense atmosphere of the weighing there was the danger that the heart itself might reveal to the gods information that could destroy its owner's hopes of reaching the afterlife. Spell 30B of the *Book of the Dead* prevented this by instructing the heart not to speak against the deceased 'in the presence of the keeper of the balance'.

Fig. 94. *Right:* Heart scarab from the mummy of King Sebekemsaf. This amulet, made of gold and jasper, is inscribed with spell 30B of the *Book of the Dead*, which commanded the heart not to betray its owner at the judgement. Thebes, 17th Dynasty, c.1590 BC. Length 3.8 cm.

enter the *Duat,* or netherworld. The passage to the afterlife was imagined as a perilous journey, during which dangers and challenges were to be overcome. Amulets provided magical protection for the deceased on this journey, and texts were placed in the tomb to equip him with ritual knowledge. These religious texts included mortuary liturgies (the words of rituals) and texts which enabled the deceased to pass through dangers and to be resurrected. The earliest collection of funerary literature, the *Pyramid Texts,* was restricted in its use to kings and members of the royal family. Later these texts became more widely accessible and were augmented with new compositions; these were mainly written on coffins and hence are now called the *Coffin Texts* (see page 83). Finally, a new set of writings emerged about 1600 BC, shortly before the New Kingdom. This selection, written predominantly on rolls of papyrus, was called by the Egyptians the 'spells for going forth by day', but is better-known today by the name the *Book of the Dead.*

These compositions, and particularly the *Book of the Dead,* reveal that the deceased's journey involved passing through many gateways, guarded by fearsome deities. The texts describe which gods the deceased would meet and explain how he should reply to their questions. At last the dead man entered the hall of judgement, where his past life was reviewed, and his heart 'weighed' to establish whether or not he truly deserved to enter the hereafter.

Following these tests the deceased attained the glorified status of *akh* and was able to enter upon the afterlife. Egyptian sources offer several different ideas of the nature of this existence and the setting in which it took place. Each probably originated as a distinct concept but by the New Kingdom it is evident that all were open to the resurrected deceased. The afterlife would be an eternal existence in close harmony with the natural phenomena of the cosmos. The cycle of sunrise and sunset would continue, and the

Fig. 93. *Pages 118-9:* The judgement of the dead. At left, Ani and his wife watch as Anubis symbolically weighs Ani's heart in a balance against a feather symbolizing Right and Truth. The ibis-headed Thoth uses a scribal palette to record that the dead man has been found free from sin. The monstrous 'Devourer', at right, waits to swallow the hearts of those who fail the test. *Book of the Dead,* papyrus of Ani. Thebes, 19th Dynasty, *c.*1275 BC. Height 42 cm.

Fig. 95. *Left:* Painted limestone shabti figure of Renseneb. He holds a vase and an *ankh* sign (signifying 'life'). On the lower body are the words of the spell which would activate the figure to work on behalf of its owner. Abydos, 13th Dynasty, *c.*1750 BC. Height 23 cm.

Fig. 96. *Right:* Blue-glazed faience shabti of King Sety I (see page 8). The figure wears the royal *nemes* headdress and holds a hoe and a mattock. The shabti text (spell 6 of the *Book of the Dead*) is inscribed on the body. Thebes, early 19th Dynasty, c.1279 BC. Height 14.5 cm.

Fig. 97. *Opposite:* Shabtis of Henutmehyt (see page 86) with wooden box, shaped like two shrines. The scene on the front depicts the dead woman adoring three of the four Sons of Horus. Thebes, 19th Dynasty, c.1250 BC. Height of box 33.5 cm.

Fig. 98. *Overleaf:* The *Book of the Dead* papyrus of Anhai. At right, the god Ptah-Sokar-Osiris sits enthroned; in the centre Anhai holds a sistrum. At the left is the Field of Reeds, an agricultural paradise where Anhai and her husband grow abundant crops and sail on the waterways of the hereafter. Thebes, 20th Dynasty, c.1100 BC. Height 42 cm.

dead, in spirit form, could travel with the sun god across the sky or dwell in the subterranean realm of Osiris. But perhaps the afterlife which most Egyptians hoped for was to live in the 'Field of Reeds', an agricultural paradise which resembled the Egypt they had known on earth, with waterways and cultivated lands in which the dead are shown ploughing, sowing and reaping abundant crops, sailing in boats and enjoying the simple pleasures of life.

The close similarities which were thought to exist between earthly life and afterlife meant that the deceased also had responsibilities. Ancient Egyptians were liable to a corvee system, by which they could be made to labour for the state. In the afterlife too, the deceased could be summoned to work in the fields of the hereafter, digging up the ground and preparing the fields for the growing of crops. To escape this duty the wealthy Egyptian took into his tomb mummy-shaped figurines called shabtis, whose role was to act as a substitute for their owner. A spell (chapter 6 of the *Book of the Dead*), often written on the body of the figure, explains that when their master should be summoned to work they are to answer 'Here I am' and to perform the tasks in his place. Many of the shabtis were depicted equipped with the tools for the job – a hoe, a mattock and a basket. With the passage of time, the importance of shabtis increased – as did their number. Whereas at first only one or two figurines per burial sufficed, in the first millennium BC it was customary to own a set of 401, a total made up of 365 'workers' (one for every day of the year) with 36 'overseers' armed with whips to keep every gang of ten workers at their tasks.

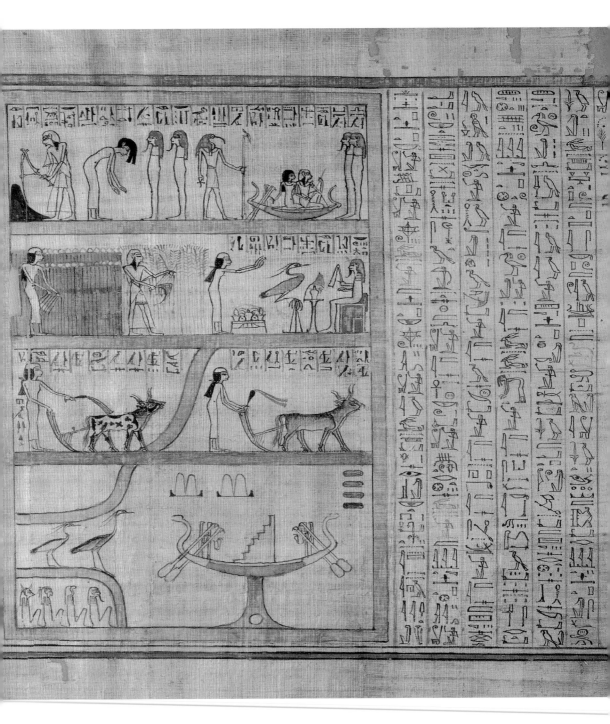

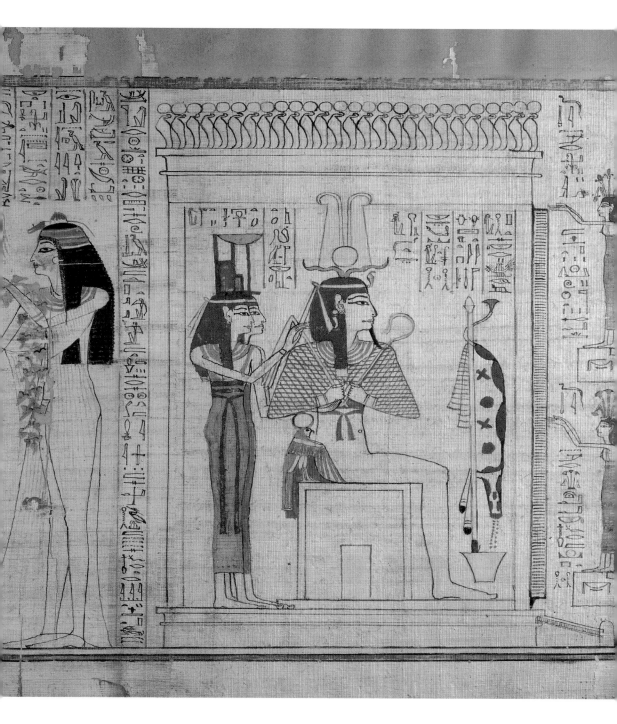

Fig. 99. *Right:*
Mummy of a young bull,
which died aged 6–12
months. The body and
limbs of the animal were
arranged on a board
which was incorporated
into the wrappings. The
horns and details of
the face are made of
coloured linen. The
geometrical patterning
is typical of animal
mummies of the Roman
Period. Thebes, after
30 BC. Height 45.7 cm.

CHAPTER 6

ANIMAL MUMMIES

Fig. 100. *Above:* Wooden box containing 'victual mummies', that were placed in the tomb as provisions for the dead. The linen-wrapped bundles contain four ducks and joints of meat, probably parts of a goat. Thebes, 19th Dynasty, c.1250 BC. Length of box 64 cm.

IN ADDITION TO THE PRESERVATION OF HUMAN REMAINS, the Egyptians devoted much attention to the mummification of animals. Animals played many varied roles in Egyptian society: they were beasts of burden, guardians, hunting companions, pets and sources of food, and they were also regarded as manifestations of the gods.

Many aspects of the Egyptians' religious beliefs were based on natural phenomena and, as part of creation, animals were linked with the divine from an early period. The distinctive characteristics of some animals were assigned to different deities, who were often depicted either wholly in animal form or as humans with the head of an animal. Hence the goddess Bastet was represented as a cat, the god Sebek as a crocodile, Thoth as an ibis or a baboon, and Taweret as a hippopotamus. The Egyptian king, who was himself of semi-divine nature, was also associated with certain powerful animals such as the bull and the lion. Because of these associations, some animals received ceremonial burial from a very early date. The remains of an elephant dating from the late Predynastic Period have been found buried in a high status cemetery at

Hierakonpolis, with the bodies of other animals (dogs, cats, a baboon) interred at the corners of a great ritual enclosure, perhaps as protectors of the sacred site. However, the large-scale mummification of animals is mainly associated with the Late Period and the Roman Period, when millions of animals, birds, reptiles and fish were embalmed and given ritual burial.

Four main types of animal mummies can be distinguished. In a few cases wealthy people had their pets mummified so that they might accompany them into the afterlife. Dogs, cats, gazelles, monkeys and baboons belonging to kings and other members of royal and elite families have been found, mainly in tombs at Thebes. Sometimes the pets were provided with painted wooden coffins or cases, fashioned in the shape of the animal enclosed within, such as the carefully embalmed Dorcas gazelle which apparently belonged to Istemkheb, a high-ranking woman of the 21st Dynasty.

Another category of preserved animal remains is that of the 'victual mummies' which provided sustenance for the dead. Geese, ducks, pigeons and joints of meat were embalmed, wrapped in linen and placed in stone or wooden boxes which were sometimes carved to reproduce the shape of the contents. Examples have been found in several tombs of high-status people, particularly of the New Kingdom. A supply of forty-eight white-painted wooden boxes containing pieces of meat was found in the antechamber of the tomb of Tutankhamun.

However, the two largest categories of animal mummies comprised creatures which were regarded as sacred. Some of these were believed to be the physical incarnation of the *ba* or spirit of a particular god (see page 11). The most famous examples are the Apis bull, which was the *ba* of the god Ptah of Memphis, and the ram of Mendes, the *ba* of the god Osiris. It was thought that only one animal could embody the god's *ba* at a given time. When this 'temple animal' died, the god was thought to have transferred his *ba* to a newly born creature (somewhat in the manner by which the Dalai Lama is believed to be reincarnated), and a search was made throughout Egypt until the new sacred animal was identified. According to the Classical writers Herodotus and Diodorus Siculus, the Apis bull could be recognized by distinctive bodily markings, including a white triangle on the forehead and an 'eagle'-shaped mark on the back. Once found, the animal was brought to live in a special temple near to that of the deity, where it was treated as a living god and carefully tended by priests. Its death was an occasion for national mourning, and its body was disposed of in a ritual manner, with an elaborate procession to the tomb. The burial places of many Apis bulls, from the reign of Amenhotep III (18th Dynasty) to that of Cleopatra VII, have been found at Saqqara. The

Fig. 101. *Right:* Round-topped sandstone stela recording the burial of a Buchis bull in the reign of the Roman emperor Diocletian, who is depicted as a Pharaoh offering to the mummified animal. From Armant AD 295. Height 76.5 cm.

Fig. 102. *Opposite:* Painted wooden coffin of a cat with white body and green head. From Bubastis, the cult centre of the cat goddess Bastet. Roman Period, after 30 BC. Height 72 cm.

remains were mummified and interred in elaborate coffins. Only a few Apis burials from the New Kingdom have been found intact, and the bodies they contained were incomplete, a strange circumstance which has led to the suggestion that these bulls might have been partially cooked and eaten, only the remnants being mummified. Later, Apis bulls were embalmed in a more conventional manner and were buried in wooden coffins and huge granite sarcophagi in a series of vaulted catacombs now known as the Serapeum.

The mummification of an Apis bull was closely modelled on the procedure used for human corpses. Massive calcite tables used for the embalming of the Apis have been discovered south-west of the temple of Ptah at Memphis. They have drainage channels and basins to collect the blood and body fluids. Perhaps because the embalming of an Apis was a rare event, the procedures used were written down and they have fortunately survived on a demotic papyrus now in Vienna. This document describes how the viscera were to be extracted (except for the heart) through an incision in the left flank, after which the cavity was to be packed with sawdust and natron in bags – both to dehydrate the corpse and to help preserve the body's shape. The body was wrapped in linen as it lay on a board, the cloth being passed through a series of metal clamps fixed along the edges. Examples of these clamps have been found in the tombs of other sacred bulls, those of Buchis, at Armant in Upper Egypt. The Buchis bulls, however, were not eviscerated via a flank incision, but by means of an infusion into the anus using an enema; bronze vessels for this operation have been discovered. The external trappings of the bulls would have included a gilded mask with eyes of glass and stone, and artificial hooves made of gold – just as human mummies were provided with a

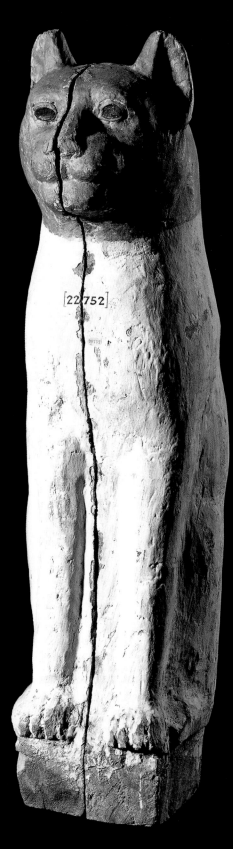

mask and with gold and silver finger and toe stalls. Another feature borrowed from human mummification was the placing of many amulets within the wrappings of temple animals. Apis and Buchis bulls and sacred rams buried at Elephantine were provided with numerous *wedjat* eyes, *djed* and *tit* amulets.

These 'temple animals' played an important role in Egyptian religious practice. Some, such as the Apis bull, acted as oracles both during their lives and after their death, and pilgrims travelled to the temples and burial places to seek the help of these creatures in obtaining recovery from sickness and solutions to other problems of everyday life. However, the fourth and final category of mummified animals fulfilled a rather different role in religious practices. During the first millennium BC there was a great increase in the desire for ways of expressing personal piety, by interacting with the gods on a one-to-one level. A popular way of doing this was to present a mummified animal at the temple as a votive offering to the gods. Thousands of cats were offered to Bastet, falcons to Horus, and ibises to Thoth – to name only three of the many deities who were honoured in this way. However, it was not thought that the god was actually present in every cat offered to Bastet or in every crocodile presented to Sebek. Instead, the creatures were supposed to act as links with the deities, intermediaries between the mortal and divine realms. In the Late Period, large numbers of these animals were evidently kept in captivity within the precincts of temples, ready to fulfil their ultimate destiny as mummies, and priests were appointed to look after their feeding and maintenance. Pilgrims regularly visited the temples and paid to offer a sacred animal to the god. The mummified creature acted as a kind of intercessor, passing on the prayers of the pilgrim to the deity. On the days of major religious

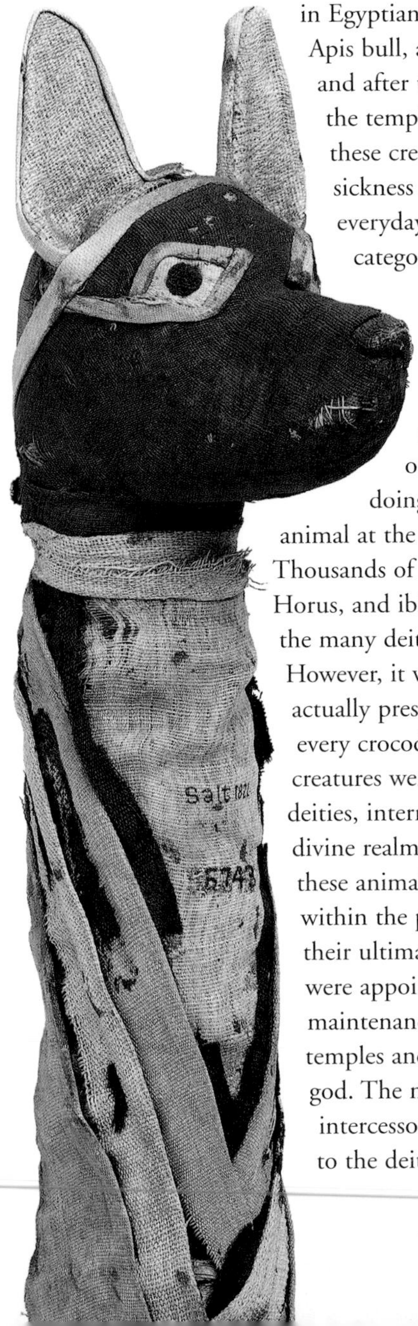

Fig. 103. *Right:* Mummy of a small dog, with a face-mask fashioned from differently coloured pieces of linen. Abydos. Roman Period, after 30 BC. Height 33.5 cm.

Fig. 104.
Left and above:
Mummified cat with
elaborate patterned
wrappings. X-rays
have shown that the
contents comprise
the remains of two
animals: the skull of a
fully mature cat and
the body of a kitten
aged 3–4 months.
Abydos. Roman
Period, after 30 BC.
Height 46 cm.

Fig. 105. *Right:* Mummy of a fish, *Anabas testudineus*, Roman Period, after 30 BC. Length 17.7 cm.

Fig. 106. *Right:* Fish-shaped wooden coffin containing a small wrapped bundle. From Akhmim, Roman Period, after 30 BC. Length 15.2 cm.

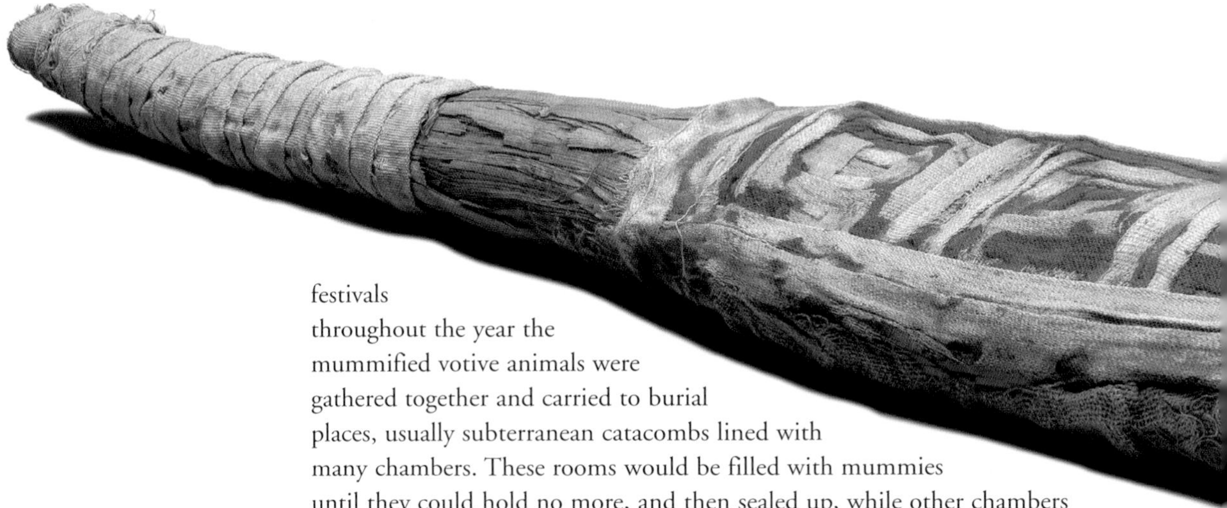

Fig. 107. *Right:* Mummy of a young crocodile with wrappings arranged in geometrical patterns. El-Hibeh, Roman Period, after 30 BC. Length 94 cm.

festivals throughout the year the mummified votive animals were gathered together and carried to burial places, usually subterranean catacombs lined with many chambers. These rooms would be filled with mummies until they could hold no more, and then sealed up, while other chambers received further mummies. It has been estimated that millions of animals were embalmed and buried in this ritual way. This practice grew enormously in scale in the Late Period and continued to be very prominent under Roman domination. The animal cults only came to an end in the late 4th century AD, when an edict of the emperor Theodosius I closed 'heathen' temples, and the Serapeum was destroyed in the reign of Honorius (AD 395–423).

As in the case of the Apis bull, the mummification method used for the more important votive animals was similar to that for human bodies: evisceration by abdominal incision or via the rectum, drying with natron, resin coating and wrapping. Often the process was simplified; the internal organs were not always extracted and the desiccation was sometimes done inefficiently. Alternative methods of preservation were also used. Thus many birds were covered with a thick coating of resin or pitch, either to compensate for inadequate drying or as a substitute for treatment with natron. Some creatures seem to have been simply dipped into hot molten resin, possibly while still alive. Finally the bodies were wrapped in linen, the outer wrappings often elaborately arranged in geometrical patterns, as was done for the mummies of humans in the Ptolemaic and Roman periods. Plaster or cartonnage masks were added to some examples.

The bodies of the animals were usually arranged in different attitudes according to the species. With the smaller creatures the aim was to make a compact bundle, and so cats and dogs were positioned as if squatting on their haunches, their front paws against the body, and the tail drawn up between the legs. Ibises were wrapped with the head bent forward and the curved beak stretched along the body. Bulls, rams and gazelles were put into a kneeling posture – an unnatural attitude which could only be achieved by cutting the tendons of the back legs. Crocodiles were fully extended. Many of these were young specimens, but fully grown adult crocodiles (some over five metres long) were also mummified. Some of these have been found with young crocodiles either positioned on their backs or in their mouths. Crocodiles carried their young in both ways in their natural state. Fish and snakes were also mummified, both individually and in groups. Even tiny creatures like beetles, lizards and shrew-mice were mummified.

Fig. 108. *Left:* Three ibis mummies wrapped in different styles. The head of the bird, with its long beak, was usually pressed tightly against the body. Upper left and right from Abydos, Roman Period, after 30 BC. Lower left from Saqqara, Ptolemaic Period (305–30 BC). Heights 35.5–43.2 cm.

Fig. 109. *Right:* Radiograph of a mummified cat, showing the typical positioning of the animal, with the forepaws placed along the front of the body. An apparent dislocation of the neck may indicate the cause of death. Roman Period, after 30 BC. Height 36.5 cm.

Fig. 110. *Below:* Bronze relic-box for the mummy of an eel. The creature is represented by the composite figure on the top, with the head of a god wearing the double crown – probably a depiction of Atum, to whom the eel was sacred. Ptolemaic Period, 305–30 BC. Length 29.8 cm.

Some animal mummies were put into containers. Ibises, in particular, were often enclosed within conical pottery jars, but other creatures could be interred in coffins of wood, stone or metal, often reproducing the shape of the animal. Another popular type of votive offering was a bronze statuette of a god, which the pilgrim presented at the temple, sometimes with a crudely carved inscription asking the deity to 'give life' to the donor. These bronze statues sometimes encased a mummified animal as well, either within the figure itself or concealed inside the rectangular plinth.

Scientific examinations of animal mummies using X-rays and CT scanning have shown that the creatures often suffered a violent death. Mummified cats usually died at under the age of twelve months. Many had been strangled or had received a heavy blow to the head, fracturing the skull. This suggests that there were periodic 'culls' of the animals to supply the demand for mummies, perhaps coinciding with religious festivals. Some young crocodiles had had their nostrils slit. How adult crocodiles were killed is unknown, but poison has been suggested as a way of disposing of these and other dangerous creatures.

Many votive animal mummies are not what they appear to be. Unwrappings and radiological examinations have revealed that some of the bundles and jars do not contain complete animals. There are bodies without heads, heads without bodies, sometimes just a few disarticulated bones, and occasionally no animal remains at all, but just sand, mud and rags. Yet the external wrappings are often carefully arranged, giving no hint of the irregularities inside. The finest cat mummy in the British Museum actually contains parts of two different cats which occupy less than half of the space within the intricately patterned wrappings. These 'fakes' may possibly have been made at times when there was a shortage of animals for mummification. It may even have been considered acceptable for a portion of the creature to take the place of the complete body (this concept of 'a part standing for the whole' was characteristic of Egyptian religious practices and iconography). Or perhaps the temple employees were simply dishonest, cheating unsuspecting pilgrims by selling them elaborately packaged bundles which contained only refuse. Whatever the reason, the large number of these ancient 'fakes' shows that the practice was widespread, and some religious officials were aware of it. The priest Hor, who worked at Saqqara in the second century BC, left an archive which reveals among other things that the arrangements for depositing animal mummies needed regulating. Hor recommended that, at least where jars containing ibises were concerned, there should be 'one god in one pot'. Still less respectful was the treatment accorded to some animal mummies just over one hundred years ago, when thousands of embalmed cats were shipped from Egypt to England to be ground into fertiliser. Fortunately, a more enlightened attitude now prevails, and through scientific research the mummies have revealed important information about the fauna of the ancient Mediterranean.

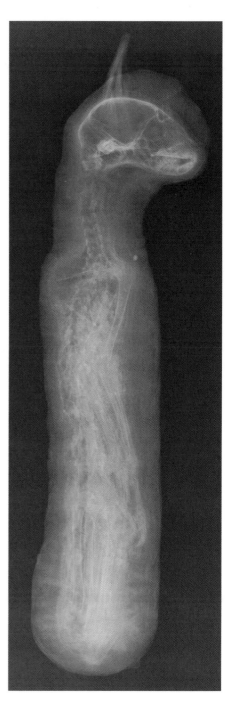

Fig. 111. *Right:*
Painting by George
Edwards 1742, of a
Ptolemaic Period
mummy from
Saqqara, which
formed part of the
collection of the
British physician
Richard Mead
(1673–1754).

CHAPTER 7

THE STUDY OF EGYPTIAN MUMMIES

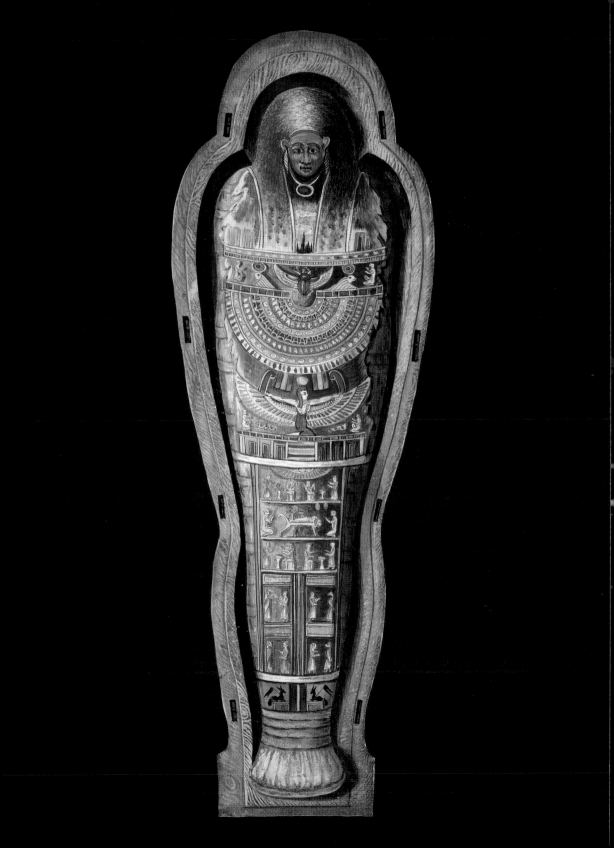

A TTITUDES TO EGYPTIAN MUMMIES have changed a great deal over the centuries. The Copts, the early Christians of Egypt, sometimes regarded them as a subject for contemplation on human mortality, but in general they left them alone. In Europe the first interest in mummies developed in a strange way.

During the Middle Ages, *mummia,* the bitumen from the Dead Sea and other parts of the Near East, was believed to possess powerful healing properties. It was, however, expensive and difficult to obtain. An acceptable substitute was found in the black tarry substances which could be extracted from the embalmed bodies of the ancient Egyptians. The term *mummia* (a word of Persian origin, also found in Arabic, meaning bitumen) was transferred to Egyptian preserved bodies, giving rise to the modern word 'mummy'. Scientific analyses have shown that bitumen was in fact rarely used in mummification, and that the dark shiny substances found in the bodies more often consisted of solidified oils and resins. But belief in their medicinal powers was strong; 'mummy' was supposed

Fig. 112. *Below:* An eighteenth century fake mummy, made from ancient linen and cartonnage and fragments of wooden coffins. These objects were made to resemble the bodies of young children. Length of coffin 49.4 cm.

to cure many ailments, and this led to a lively trade in embalmed bodies, which were ground to powder. Its use as a medicament is described as early as the twelfth century by the Andalusian geographer Al-Zohri, and though some scholars disapproved of its widespread use, there was a demand for it among members of the elite in Europe. The French king Francis I habitually carried a sachet containing powdered mummy in case he should have need of an urgent remedy. By the sixteenth century European apothecaries were obtaining large quantities of the drug from Egypt. Demand outstripped supply, and this led to the creation of fake mummies. Guy de la Fontaine, physician to the King of Navarre, visited Alexandria in 1564 and found that traders were fabricating 'mummies' from the unclaimed bodies of persons who had recently died, or even from the corpses of executed criminals.

The use of mummy as a drug slowly waned, and had largely come to an end in Europe by the nineteenth century. In the meantime attitudes to the ancient bodies had changed. The more intrepid European travellers of the seventeenth and eighteenth centuries visited Egypt and began to explore the tombs. Some of them brought mummies home as souvenirs, and they began to be regarded as 'curiosities', objects of antiquarian interest which could reveal information about the society and culture of the ancient Egyptians. Men of learning displayed them in their private collections or 'cabinets', the forerunners of modern museums (see fig. 11, page 21). Interest focussed particularly on the coffins and trappings, which were covered with still-mysterious images and inscriptions, but in the eighteenth century the hieroglyphs could not be read and Egyptian history was mainly filtered through Classical sources, often inaccurate or incomplete. Without a historical framework into which new information could be fitted, scholarly enquiry into mummies could not be effectively directed.

Napoleon's expedition to Egypt in 1798 marked the birth of Egyptology. The discovery of the Rosetta Stone (see page 157) by French troops led to the decipherment of hieroglyphic script, and this in turn opened the vast store of the ancient Egyptians' own writings, enabling the political and social history of the land to be recovered. Scholarly records of monuments were made and collections of antiquities were formed, contributing greatly to this advance in knowledge. Mummies were among the most avidly collected items, not only as objects of curiosity in themselves but because papyri, amulets and jewellery were often found within their wrappings. From the 1810s to the 1830s, large collections of antiquities were amassed by European diplomats and travellers in Egypt, some of which eventually formed the basis of major museum collections. To supply the demand for objects there was much indiscriminate digging at

THE MUMMY PITS

Searching for mummies was often a dangerous and exhausting experience. The Italian explorer Giovanni Belzoni (1778–1823) left a graphic description of a visit to the 'mummy pits' on the Theban west bank where he searched for papyri among the heaps of bodies:

'After getting through these passages, some of them two or three hundred yards long, you generally find a more commodious place, perhaps high enough to sit. But what a place of rest! Surrounded by bodies, by heaps of mummies in all directions; which, previous to my being accustomed to the sight, impressed me with horror … Once I was conducted from such a place to another resembling it, through a passage of about twenty feet in length, and no wider than that a body could be forced through. It was choked with mummies, and I could not pass without putting my face in contact with that of some decayed Egyptian; but as the passage inclined downwards, my own weight helped me on: however, I could not avoid being covered with bones, legs, arms, and heads rolling from above.'

Fig. 113. *Above:* Portrait of Giovanni Battista Belzoni (1778–1823), one of the most celebrated European explorers of Egypt in the early nineteenth century.

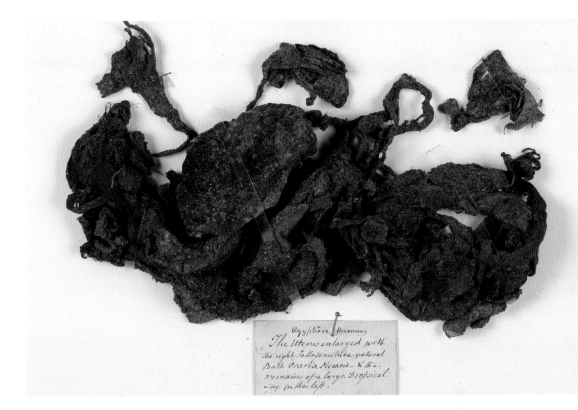

Fig. 114. *Above:* Uterus of a female mummy, autopsied in London by A. B. Granville. The rounded object at centre left is an ovarian tumour. The label below forms part of the original display of the mummy parts prepared by Granville in 1821. Thebes, 26th Dynasty, c.550 BC. Length 21 cm.

ancient sites, both by the local inhabitants and by agents of European collectors.

Deceptions were practiced on some collectors. The suppliers often transposed the mummies and coffins of different persons in order to create a more attractive 'package' for buyers. There were even fake mummies, a number of which were sold to collectors as early as the mid-eighteenth century. These were often small mummies, purporting to be those of young children, wrapped in bandages and adorned with ancient pieces of cartonnage (fig. 112, page 142). But those which have been opened or X-rayed contained only odd bones, animal remains or rubbish. The most outrageous example of this practice was the 'bearded mummy', allegedly sold to an English collector as a great rarity in the 1820s. It was in fact the corpse of a European who had died in Egypt a few years earlier and had become naturally mummified by being buried in the sand.

The flood of mummies into Europe led to a craze for unwrapping them. In England this seems to have been launched by Belzoni, who staged a very

Fig. 115. *Right:* Cartonnage mummy case which contained the remains of a child who suffered from the rare condition known as brittle bone disease (*osteogenesis imperfecta*). The addition of a sun disc and ostrich feathers as a headdress to the mummy-case may have been intended to emphasize the identification of the child with the god Osiris. From Speos Artemidos, near Beni Hasan. 22nd Dynasty, *c.*800 BC. Height of coffin 73 cm.

popular exhibition of his discoveries in London in 1821 and unwrapped three mummies. In the following decades many more such investigations took place, often as publicly staged performances which attracted large audiences. The worst of these events merely satisfied morbid curiosity, but others were aimed at gathering scientific data. Thomas Joseph Pettigrew (1791–1865), a London doctor, was the most distinguished 'unroller' of mummies at the time. He sometimes resorted to harsh methods (including the use of crowbars) to penetrate the solidified resin-soaked bandages, but his studies were directed towards establishing the methods which the ancient embalmers had used. He published his findings in 1834 in a book which is still of value to researchers today. Another surgeon, the Italian-born Augustus Bozzi Granville, conducted an extremely careful unwrapping and dissection of a mummy in 1821, using all the scientific techniques available at the time. The specimens of skin, bone, and internal organs which he prepared as exhibits are in the collections of the British Museum; they include an ovarian tumour, which is the oldest example of this complaint so far discovered (see fig. 114, page 145).

After the 1830s the investigation of mummies waned in Europe. The limits of what could be learned from the methods available at the time had been reached, and the tightening of the laws governing the export of Egyptian antiquities had reduced the supply of mummies. Hopes of finding the bodies of historical personages such as Alexander the Great or Cleopatra had been disappointed. The pyramids and the royal tombs in the Valley of the Kings had been investigated, and all had been found plundered. The mummies of the pharaohs, it was supposed, had been destroyed by ancient robbers.

Then came an astonishing discovery. In 1881 Emile Brugsch of the Egyptian antiquities service was shown a hidden tomb in the cliffs of Deir el-Bahri on the Theban west bank. It had been discovered about ten years earlier by the local Abdel-Rassul family, who had kept their find a secret, and it contained the mummies of ten pharaohs of the New Kingdom, together with those of many members of their families. Among the kings were some of the most famous: Ahmose I, Amenhotep I, Tuthmosis III, Sety I and Ramesses II. In 1898 another group, including Tuthmosis IV and Amenhotep III, was found in a side-room in the tomb of Amenhotep II. Most of the mummies lay in rough, plain coffins (often second-hand ones) and little or nothing remained of the jewellery and rich trappings which had originally accompanied them. Terse, businesslike notes written in ink on the coffins and mummy wrappings explained how they had come to rest in these communal burial places: at the end of the New Kingdom state officials had dismantled the royal burials of the Theban necropolis, recycling the precious metals and stones to save them from

Fig. 116. *Above:* The mummy of King Seqenenre Tao, showing multiple wounds to the forehead and face, inflicted by an axe and a dagger or spear. From Deir el-Bahri, 17th Dynasty, c.1560 BC. Height 1.7 m.

robbers and to reinvigorate Egypt's struggling economy. The bodies had been transferred from tomb to tomb over a period of about 150 years before reaching their final resting-places.

The royal mummies were taken to Cairo, and most of them were unwrapped, often very quickly and without a full record being made. Several of the mummies turned out to have been badly damaged by robbers, and uncertainty hovers over the identity of some of the remains. Nevertheless, they offered a unique opportunity to confront major historical figures from the remote past, face-to-face, as well as providing a valuable series of well-dated examples of the development of mummification techniques. One of the most unexpected findings was that King Seqenenre Tao had died violently, his head covered with wounds (fig. 116). He had ruled over a limited territory in the 17th Dynasty, at a time when the Delta was controlled by the Asiatic Hyksos, and Upper Egypt was suffering raids and attacks from a powerful Nubian state to the south. One of the few written sources to mention Seqenenre is a story in which he receives a complaint from the Hyksos ruler about the noise made by hippopotami at Thebes (about 650 km away from the Hyksos city of Avaris), evidently a pretext for conflict. While the story may not be 'history', it preserves a tradition that there was a confrontation between these rulers, and the discovery that Seqenenre had suffered a traumatic death provides a vital clue to understanding the events of the time.

The royal bodies were examined in detail by the anatomist Grafton Elliot Smith, who at the beginning of the twentieth century was the leading figure in the study of Egyptian mummies. At the same period important advances in mummy research were made. Alfred Lucas investigated the chemical processes of embalming by analysing natron and other preservatives found on mummies and in embalmer's caches. Marc Armand Ruffer subjected mummies to the techniques of histology, by which thin slices of soft tissue, rehydrated and chemically stained, can reveal details of their structures and abnormalities (such as microorganisms responsible for disease) under the microscope. This work continues to the present day, but necessarily involves at least partial unwrapping of the bodies and sometimes their dissection.

Since the 1960s the emergence of new scientific techniques and the adoption of a multidisciplinary approach have transformed the investigation of mummies. Research has focussed on anthropology, nutrition, health and disease in ancient Egypt, on genetic evidence and on the search for a better understanding of the processes of mummification. It is now realized that mummies hold a vast amount of information on these subjects and that they are all the more valuable because they illuminate aspects of Egyptian society and culture which have left relatively little trace in the written record.

To obtain this information, an armoury of scientific techniques is now available, many of which have been adapted from the field of modern medicine. Because mummies are a finite and valuable resource, which can be damaged by unwrapping, emphasis is placed on non-invasive methods of study. Advances in imaging have greatly extended the amount of data which can be obtained in this way. Conventional X-rays have been applied to mummies since the 1890s and provide excellent images of the skeletal structure. Although this basic technique is still used, computed tomography (CT) scanning has become more widespread, allowing the collection of very detailed images of what lies inside a wrapped body. This method enables a much more precise distinction to be made between bones, soft tissues and wrappings, as well as defining objects either intentionally or unintentionally placed under the bandages by the embalmers. The technique also enables three-dimensional images to be created and provides the means of making facial reconstructions based on the shape of the skull. However, care is needed in interpreting CT images, as the density of body tissues in mummified remains may differ significantly from those in recent specimens. Where access to the surface of the body is possible, medical endoscopes can sometimes be inserted to explore the internal cavities and to reveal preserved organs and traces of embalming substances or packing materials.

Invasive studies continue but these now rarely involve the complete dissection of a corpse, as was sometimes done in the nineteenth and twentieth centuries. Instead small tissue samples are retrieved and are used as the basis of chemical, histological and molecular studies. The blood groups of some mummies have been identified, and this method revealed that Tutankhamun had the same blood group as a royal mummy found in tomb 55 in the Valley of the Kings, which some Egyptologists believe is the body of the 'heretic' pharaoh Akhenaten.

The retrieval of ancient DNA from Egyptian mummies was first announced by Svante Pääbo in 1985. DNA holds the potential to reveal much about the origins and ethnic profile of the ancient Egyptians, their relationships with other ancient populations and the family connections of specific individuals, notably the pharaohs of the New Kingdom. However, the DNA recovered has been small in quantity and poorly preserved, indicating that great age, burial conditions and perhaps mummification processes cause its degradation. Mummies are also vulnerable to contamination with the DNA of people who have come into contact with them both in antiquity and in modern times. For these reasons progress in this field has been slow, and it remains to be seen how many key questions ancient DNA can answer. The DNA of parasites, bacteria and viruses has also been identified in mummies, throwing important light on the incidence of ancient diseases.

Scientific research on mummies has opened a world of information about living conditions, health and disease in ancient Egypt. Medical texts on papyri

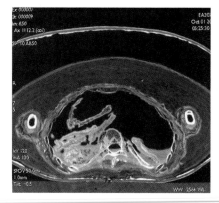

Fig. 117. *Right:* Cross-sectional CT 'slice' through a wrapped mummy, showing the cartonnage case, multiple layers of linen wrappings, and linen bundles and solidified resin inside the body cavity. Thebes, 22nd Dynasty, *c.*800 BC.

provide data about some of the ailments the Egyptians suffered from and reveal the extent of their medical knowledge and treatments available to them, but the human remains preserve a medical museum of case histories. From these remains it is clear that arthritis, tuberculosis, smallpox and arteriosclerosis were all present and that parasitic diseases were especially common. Tapeworms have been found and the calcified eggs of the

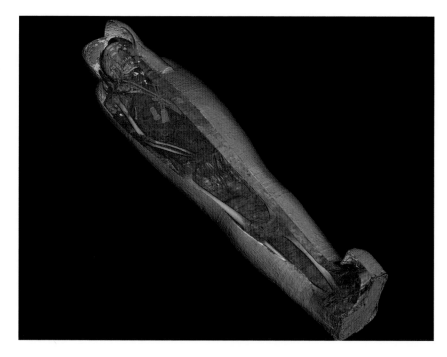

Fig. 118. *Left:* Three-dimensional cutaway image of the mummy of Nesperennub (fig. 48, page 58), based on CT data. Within the cartonnage case and the wrappings, the bones and the amulets placed on the body have been selectively illustrated. Thebes, 22nd Dynasty, c.800 BC.

schistosoma are seen in internal organs, showing that schistosomiasis (bilharzia) was endemic. External parasites such as lice have been found in hair. Histological studies of lung tissue from canopic containers have revealed traces of several complaints, including sand pneumoconiosis and anthracosis (caused by inhaling tiny particles of sand and soot during life) and emphysema. Bones reveal much evidence of trauma (fractures of all kinds, healed and unhealed) showing that many Egyptians received injuries in life, some of which were fatal. Examination of teeth has contributed to knowledge of ancient diet and also provides important clues to the age at which Egyptians died. The teeth of ancient Egyptians show heavy wear caused by the grit with which bread was contaminated. This wear often exposed the roots of the teeth and led to infections; many mummies, even those of persons of high status, reveal severe dental abscesses, some of which could have proved fatal.

The modern study of mummies continues to yield invaluable information about the methods used by the embalmers in preserving bodies: the manipulations and operations they performed to extract organs, the materials used in preservation and in packing the body, and the manner in which the bodies were 'beautified' and wrapped.

The future of mummy investigation lies in the greater coordination of

Fig. 119. *Right:* Encaustic portrait on a limewood panel, from the mummy of a woman. Her clothing, hairstyle and jewellery (gold ball-earrings and necklace with crescent-shaped pendant) are characteristic of the reign of the Roman emperor Nero. From Hawara, AD 55–70. Height 41.6 cm.

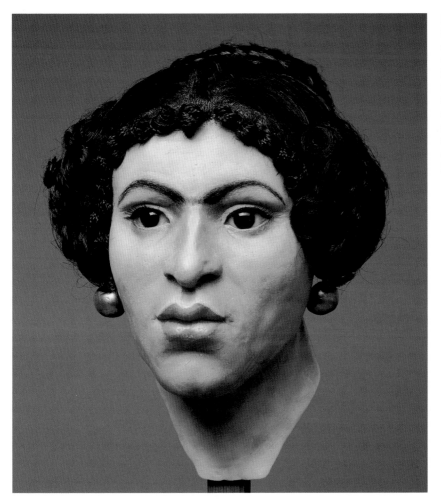

Fig. 120. *Left:* Reconstruction of the face of the woman depicted in fig. 119 opposite. The facial features were manually rebuilt over a cast of the skull, and the hairstyle and jewellery based on the details of the portrait.

strategies for study and more effective ways of recording findings and presenting new information coherently. Scientific examinations can now be carried out in the field as part of the excavation process, as well as in the museum and laboratory. A centralized international mummy tissue bank has been established to house samples of mummified tissue for research. Besides throwing light on living conditions in the past, mummy research can also benefit present-day society. Tracing the historic development of a disease found in a mummy can improve understanding of its evolution and hence can offer clues to help combat it with greater chances of success. In this way, as in many other aspects of life, modern man continues to learn from the ancient Egyptians.

Chronology

All dates before 690 BC are approximate.

PRE-DYNASTIC PERIOD	5500–3100 BC
Badarian period	5500–4000 BC
Amratian (Naqada I) period	4000–3500 BC
Gerzean (Naqada II) period	3500–3100 BC
EARLY DYNASTIC PERIOD	3100–2686 BC
1st Dynasty	3100–2890 BC
2nd Dynasty	2890–2686 BC
OLD KINGDOM	2686–2181 BC
3rd Dynasty	2686–2613 BC
4th Dynasty	2613–2494 BC
5th Dynasty	2494–2345 BC
6th Dynasty	2345–2181 BC
FIRST INTERMEDIATE PERIOD	2181–2055 BC
7th and 8th Dynasties	2181–2125 BC
9th and 10th Dynasties	
(Herakleopolitan)	2160–2025 BC
11th Dynasty (Thebes only)	2125–2055 BC
MIDDLE KINGDOM	2055–1650 BC
11th Dynasty (All Egypt)	2055–1985 BC
12th Dynasty	1985–1795 BC
13th Dynasty	1795–after 1650 BC
14th Dynasty	1750–1650 BC
SECOND INTERMEDIATE PERIOD	1650–1550 BC
15th Dynasty (Hyksos)	1650–1550 BC
16th–17th Dynasties	1650–1550 BC

NEW KINGDOM	1550–1069 BC
18th Dynasty	1550–1295 BC
19th Dynasty	1295–1186 BC
20th Dynasty	1186–1069 BC
THIRD INTERMEDIATE PERIOD	1069–747 BC
21st Dynasty (Tanite)	1069–945 BC
22nd Dynasty (Bubastite/Libyan)	945–715 BC
23rd Dynasty (Tanite/Libyan)	818–715 BC
24th Dynasty	727–715 BC
LATE PERIOD	747–332 BC
25th Dynasty (Kushite)	747–656 BC
26th Dynasty (Saite)	664–525 BC
27th Dynasty (First Persian Period)	525–404 BC
28th Dynasty	404–399 BC
29th Dynasty	399–380 BC
30th Dynasty	380–343 BC
31st Dynasty (Second Persian Period)	343–332 BC
PTOLEMAIC PERIOD	332–30 BC
Macedonian Dynasty	332–305 BC
Ptolemaic Dynasty	305–30 BC
ROMAN PERIOD	30 BC–AD 395

Further reading

Assmann, Jan, *Death and Salvation in Ancient Egypt* (Ithaca and London, 2005).

Aufderheide, Arthur, *The Scientific Study of Mummies* (Cambridge, 2003).

D'Auria, Sue, Lacovara, Peter and Roehrig, Catharine H. (eds), *Mummies & Magic: The Funerary Arts of Ancient Egypt* (Boston, 1988).

David, Rosalie (ed.), *Egyptian Mummies and Modern Science* (Cambridge, 2008).

Dunand, Francoise and Lichtenberg, Roger, *Mummies and Death in Egypt* (Ithaca and London, 2006).

Forman, Werner and Quirke, Stephen, *Hieroglyphs and the Afterlife in Ancient Egypt* (London, 1996).

Grajetzki, Wolfram, *Burial Customs in Ancient Egypt: Life in Death for Rich and Poor* (London, 2003).

Ikram, Salima (ed.), *Divine Creatures: Animal Mummies in Ancient Egypt* (Cairo and New York, 2005).

Ikram, Salima and Dodson, Aidan, *The Mummy in Ancient Egypt* (London, 1998).

Taylor, John H., *Death and the Afterlife in Ancient Egypt* (London, 2001).

Web resources

The British Museum registration numbers for the individual objects illustrated in this book are listed on page 160. You can find out more about objects in all areas of the British Museum collections on the museum website at www.britishmuseum.org.

For online tours of the Egyptian galleries visit: www.britishmuseum.org/explore/online_tours.aspx

To explore the collections database of more than 1,800,000 objects, visit: www.british museum.org/research/search_the_collection_database.aspx

Glossary

Akh A transfigured spirit: the perfect state of existence which the dead would attain in the afterlife.

Amulet A natural or man-made object, believed to be endowed with magical power to give special abilities or protection to the owner.

Anthropoid coffin Coffin in the shape of a human body.

Anubis God who protected the dead and was responsible for mummification; usually depicted in the form of a black dog or jackal, or as a man with the head of that animal.

Ba Spirit aspect of a living or dead person, often equated with the notion of the 'soul'. The *ba* was usually depicted as a human-headed bird; in this form a dead person was able to leave the tomb and return to the world of the living.

Bitumen Naturally-occurring tarry substance found in the Dead Sea and other areas; used by the ancient Egyptians in mummification.

Book of the Dead Modern title for the collection of about 200 magical spells which the Egyptians called the *Book of Coming Forth by Day*. These texts provided the dead with knowledge and special powers to assist them in their passage to the afterlife. Usually written on papyrus rolls, they were used from about 1600 BC to the first century BC.

Canopic jars Sets of four vessels which contained parts of the preserved internal organs of the corpse – usually the liver, lungs, stomach and intestines. The lids of the jars often depicted the heads of deities called the Sons of Horus.

Cartonnage A lightweight and malleable material made from layers of linen, glue and plaster; often used to make funerary masks and mummy-cases.

Coffin Texts Collection of over 1000 magical spells for the use of the dead; usually inscribed on the surfaces of rectangular wooden coffins made for persons of high status, chiefly in the Middle Kingdom.

Coptic/Copts Name given to the early Christian population of Egypt; derived from the Greek name for Egypt, *Aigyptios*. The term Coptic also denotes the last stage of the ancient Egyptian language.

Desiccation The process of drying; in Egyptian mummification this was usually achieved by the use of natron salts.

Djed A pillar – perhaps originally a tree or plant – which came to be identified with the god Osiris, and specifically as his backbone. Amulets in this form denoted stability.

Duat Ancient Egyptian name for the Netherworld, ruled over by Osiris.

Evisceration Removal of the internal organs from a body.

False door A sculptural representation of a panelled doorway, usually installed in the cult-place of a tomb. The spirit of the deceased was supposed to pass through the door in order to receive food-offerings.

Hery seshta 'He who is over the secrets'; ancient Egyptian title of the chief of the embalmers.

Hypocephalus 'Under the head' (Greek): modern name for an amulet consisting of an inscribed disc of linen, which created a life-giving flame beneath the head of a mummy.

Ibu or *ibu en wab* Ancient Egyptian term for the tent-like structure in which the cleansing of the corpse was performed, prior to mummification.

Incantation A magical spell or recitation to be spoken aloud.

Ka Spirit aspect of a person. After death it dwelt in the tomb and was sustained with offerings. The *ka* was depicted either as a 'double' of its owner or as a pair of upraised arms.

Khery-hebet Ancient Egyptian term for a lector priest, one who read sacred texts from a papyrus roll.

Maat The ancient Egyptian concept of Order, Right and Truth, often personified as a goddess, the daughter of the sun-god Ra.

Natron Naturally occurring compound of salts – usually consisting chiefly of sodium carbonate and sodium bicarbonate; used as a drying agent in mummification.

Netherworld The realm of the dead.

Nut Goddess who personified the sky; she was also the mother of Osiris and in Egyptian funerary texts is often referred to as the eternal mother of the deceased.

Osiris God, supposedly a king in the mythical past, who was murdered by his brother Seth and later restored to life. He became ruler of the Netherworld and judge of the dead.

Per-nefer 'Beautiful House' or 'House of Rejuvenation': ancient Egyptian term for the place of mummification.

Pyramid Texts Magical spells inscribed on the walls of the internal chambers of pyramids in the late Old Kingdom, to assist the dead king to reach the afterlife.

Ra The sun-god; often associated with the god Horus and depicted as a man with the head of a falcon.

Resin Sticky, semi-transparent extract from plants and trees, used by the Egyptians to make incense and also applied to the bodies of the dead during mummification.

Rishi coffins Anthropoid coffins of the period 1700–1500 BC, decorated with a design of large wings (from an Arabic term, meaning 'feather').

Rosetta Stone A granite-like stela (or tablet) bearing a royal decree of Ptolemy V in three scripts – Egyptian hieroglyphic, Egyptian demotic and ancient Greek. Discovered at Rosetta in 1799, it provided European scholars with the key to the decipherment of Egyptian hieroglyphs.

Sah Ancient Egyptian term for a mummy.

Sarcophagus Large coffin, usually made of stone, serving as the outer container for the corpse.

Scarab Carved representation of the dung beetle *Scarabaeus sacer*. The scarab beetle was regarded as a manifestation of the sun god at dawn. As an amulet it also conveyed protection to the deceased – particularly to his/her heart.

Senetjer Ancient Egyptian word for incense, literally 'that which makes divine'. The substance used (often *pistacia* resin) was also employed in mummification.

Serdab A concealed chamber within a tomb which contained one or more statues of the dead person. From an Arabic word for 'cellar'.

Shabti Ancient Egyptian term for a statuette of a dead person, usually in mummy form; it acted as a substitute for its owner to carry out agricultural tasks for him/her in the afterlife.

Tit Ancient Egyptian term for the 'Isis knot', an amulet associated with the blood of Isis, which conferred the goddess' protection on the owner.

Wabet 'Pure place' or 'place of purification': ancient Egyptian term for the place of mummification.

Wedjat (or Wedjat-eye) Ancient Egyptian term for the eye of the god Horus, which, in mythology, was injured and afterwards healed. It became a powerful protective amulet.

Wesekh Ancient Egyptian term for an amuletic collar, often placed on a mummy or depicted on the mummy mask or coffin.

Wet Ancient Egyptian term for an embalmer.

Index Page numbers in *italic* refer to illustrations/captions

British Museum registration numbers

Fig.	Reg. no.
1	EA 6666
3	EA 10554/17
4	EA 65206
5	EA 9900/6
6	EA 9900/6
7	EA 24792
8	EA 10541
9	EA 1162
10	EA 9980
12	EA 9901/1
15	EA 1482
16	EA 32751
18	EA 24957
19	EA 43218
20	EA 20728, 21952, 23326, 23351, 26409, 49594-5
22	EA 67815
23	EA 6665
24	EA 22814
25	EA 22939
26	EA 15572
27	EA 6704
28	EA 13595
29	EA 6707
30	EA 15717-8
31	EA 683
32	EA 29996
33	EA 29770
34	EA 29472
35	EA 69020
36	EA 26799
37	EA 21810
38	EA 26273A
39	EA 30838
40	EA 59197-59200
41	EA 10561
42	EA 15563-4, 15573, 15576
43	EA 30720
45	EA 6682
46	EA 10098/11
47	EA 71492
48	EA 14594-5
49	EA 41668
50	EA 14703, 52847, 14622, 30416
51	EA 20639
52	EA 12196
53	EA 10470/33
54	EA 55265
55	EA 60824, 11291, 61035, 29983, 60507
56	EA 7865
57	EA 6714
58	EA 36188
59	EA 54244-7
60	EA 41572
61	EA 52888
62	EA 71620
63	EA 30839
64	EA 6652
65	EA 1001
66	EA 48001
67	EA 24792
68	EA 22939
69	EA 20744
70	EA 29577
71	EA 75193
72	EA 17
73	EA 22940
74	EA 15655, 27735
75	EA 24906
76	EA 6693
77	EA 29776
78	EA 10
79	EA 29585
80	EA 6705
81	EA 26273
83	EA 10470/5
84	EA 9901/5
85	EA 5526
86	EA 30718
89	EA 32610
90	EA 2371
91	EA 9861
92	EA 9525
93	EA 10470/3
94	EA 7876
95	EA 49343
96	EA 22818
97	EA 41548
98	EA 10472/5
99	EA 6773
100	EA 51812
101	EA 1696
102	EA 22752
103	EA 6743
104	EA 37348
105	EA 24647
106	EA 20764
107	EA 37347
108	EA 52926, 68219, 53938
109	EA 6758
110	EA 36151
112	EA 6952
114	EA 75991
115	EA 41603
117	EA 30720
118	EA 30720
119	EA 74713

Picture credits

Fig. 2: © Katz Pictures.

Fig. 11: © Photo: akg-images / De Agostini Picture Library.

Figs 13 and 14: © Roemer-und Pelizaeus-Museum Hildesheim (Germany); photo: Shahrok Shalchi.

Fig. 17: *Strand Magazine* XI (1896), p. 68.

Fig. 21: Reproduced from *A Contribution to the Study of Mummification*, by G. Elliot Smith, pl. III.

Fig. 44: © The Trustees of the British Museum; CT scan: IMA Solutions Ltd, Toulouse, France.

Fig. 82: © The Trustees of the British Museum; facsimile by Nina Davies.

Figs 87 and 88: Drawn by Claire Thorne.

Fig. 113: © The British Library Board.

Fig. 116: © Getty Images.

Fig. 117: © The Trustees of the British Museum; CT scan: The National Hospital for Neurology and Neurosurgery, London.

Fig. 118: © The Trustees of the British Museum; photo: IMA Solutions Ltd, Toulouse, France.

All other images in this book are © The Trustees of the British Museum.